Motivational Units
For Fall

Written by
Susanne Glover and Georgeann Grewe

Illustrated by
Georgeann Grewe

Cover by Janet Skiles

Copyright © Good Apple, Inc., 1990

Good Apple, Inc.
1204 Buchanan St., Box 299
Carthage, IL 62321-0299

Copyright © Good Apple, Inc., 1990

ISBN No. 0-86653-543-8

Printing No. 987654321

Good Apple, Inc.
1204 Buchanan St., Box 299
Carthage, IL 62321-0299

Dedication

Dedicated to these special children who touch and inspire our lives.

Trisha

Sarah

Ronnie

Debbie

Jeremy

Craig

Monica

Aaron

Adam

Aric

Michael

Tina

Anne

Joshua

Fred

Heather

Melissa

Kim

Ronnie

GA1146

TABLE OF CONTENTS

GA1146

DRESS FOR SUCCESS

Preparing yourself and your classroom to make those good impressions is the first step toward starting the school year off right. Children will be challenged and motivated by you and the atmosphere you create in your classroom.

In this section you will find attractive decorations to color your room, not only for fall, but throughout the following months. Simply change captions and use the bulletin board ideas for other seasons/content areas.

1

GA1146

BULLETIN BOARDS

The Finish Line

Batter Up

JOSH

ANNE

BRAGGIN' TRAIN

ADMIT ONE

STEVE JILL RON ANN SUE

2

for FALL

Let me HAND it
to you

1st Class Students

Barb

Bill

SCENTsational !

3

GA1146

NAME

MOBILEIZE YOUR ROOM

Nickname: _____

Birthday: _____

Hobbies: _____
_____

Friends: _____
_____
_____

With proper nutrition your students will blossom into the academic and social citizens we hope they will be. The activities in this unit will nurture them in the many phases of the curriculum, providing combinations of individual and group work as well as structured and relaxed learning strategies. Bite into the unit and let the fun begin!

FOOD for THOUGHT

5

GA1146

Materials:
    Yellow paper for background
    Green paper for lettering
    Large sheet of poster board for the large apple core person
    Black, red and green construction paper for the smaller apple core people
    Sturdy white paper for the apple art lesson (patterns on page 7)
    White paper for the writing lesson (see page 8)

Directions:
1. Place the lettering and large apple core person on the bulletin board.
2. Give each child the apple core pattern and colored construction paper to create the apple core person. Remind students to write their names on the backs of their art projects.
3. Next, give each child writing paper. Suggested writing activities include a) Pretend that you are the apple person. Write a story about yourself. b) Write a poem about the apple person. c) Copy your favorite apple recipe on the paper or create a "Recipe for a Good Year." d) Research a topic related to apples and summarzie your findings on the paper—Johnny Appleseed, types of apples, uses of apples, etc.
4. Display finished projects on the bulletin board.

APPLE PERSON

7

GA1146

 GA1146

THE APPLE BLOSSOMS

Just as an apple grows from one tiny seed, so, too, does a paragraph. The seed is like an idea that will blossom into something fun to write and read.

Now let's begin and I will help you. Our *seed* or idea is an *apple*. I will ask you a few questions. Answer them in complete sentences.

1. What did the apple look like? _____
   _____

2. Why was it lonely? _____
   _____

3. How did the apple show its loneliness? _____
   _____

4. When was it the loneliest? _____
   _____

Now copy your answers from above and plant them on the lines below in your best handwriting. Watch your story grow!

   High in an old, crooked tree grew an apple. _____
_____
_____
_____
_____
_____
_____
_____
_____

9

GA1146

Your story is growing! Dig around now and let's plant another *seed*. This time we are thinking about a *worm*. Answer the questions below in complete sentences. Be sure to choose words that say exactly what you want.

1. What did the worm look like? _____

_____

2. How did the bark of the tree feel to the worm? _____

_____

3. What was the worm doing? _____

_____

4. What did the worm want? _____

_____

Now copy your answers from above and plant them on the lines below in your best handwriting. Watch your story grow!

Slowly up the tree trunk crawled a worm. _____

_____

_____

_____

_____

_____

_____

_____

_____

_____

_____

_____

GA1146

Your story now is germinating. If you take care of your seeds and water them well, you will have a healthy plant.

Now let's plant one last seed. Think about the idea of an apple and a worm meeting each other for the first time. Answer questions in complete sentences.

1. What did the worm do? _____

_____

2. What did the apple do? _____

_____

3. Was the apple still lonely? _____

_____

4. What happened? _____

_____

Copy your answers from above on the lines below in your best writing. You are getting very good at this!

   It began to rain very hard and the scraggly, twisted tree began to shake.

_____

_____

_____

_____

_____

_____

_____

_____

_____

_____

Your story is about to bloom. Read your paragraphs at the bottom of pages 9, 10 and 11. As carefully as you can, copy those three paragraphs in order on the lines below. Be sure to use capital letters and correct punctuation.

The Lonely Apple

High in an old, crooked tree grew an apple. _____

_____

_____

_____

_____

_____

Slowly up the tree trunk crawled a worm._____

_____

_____

_____

_____

_____

It began to rain very hard and the scraggly, twisted tree began to shake. _____

_____

_____

_____

_____

Did you notice that your story had three *seeds* or ideas? Those are the parts that I wrote in for you. I indented each paragraph so that you could see where each seed was planted.

You are truly a budding author. Reread your story on page 12. Now read it again, but this time, use your pencil to check your work. Use the questions below to help you.

1. Did I start each sentence with a capital letter?
2. Did I use periods, question marks, and other punctuation where needed?
3. Did I indent each paragraph?
4. Did I spell my words correctly?
5. Do I need to change any words to make my feelings clearer or my story better?

If you are pleased with your work, copy your story for the last time on the lines below. Be sure to include all of your corrections.

Your *seed* has grown. You planted it and watered it so that it would blossom. What a fine work of art you have created!

GA1146

FUN FRUIT RELAYS

It's time for some fun! Below are just a few activities to try with your class. Use the ideas as suggested, or vary them to meet the needs of your classroom.

1. **Apple Turnover**—Divide the class into teams. Students are to lie flat, stretching out. Have them roll from one end of the room to the other, and then roll back to their team. The next student follows.

2. **Apple Jacks**—This is an individual activity. Perform it similar to a jumping jack, except cross feet on the bounces. You may also want to use an arm variation.

3. **Bushel of Fun**—Divide the class into teams. At the head of each team place a bushel basket (or clothes basket). Cut out several construction paper apples, or you may want to use real apples. Place the apples in the basket at the opposite end of the room. At the sound of the whistle, have each team send a player, running, to get an apple from the basket and then run back to the end of the line. After all players on the team have gotten an apple, the first player must then run to the basket and return his apple. The first team to accomplish this, wins.

4. **Wiggle Worm**—This relay may be done in several ways. Choose one appropriate to your grade level. First, have children "inch" their way to the opposite end of the room and back using a crawling motion on the floor. Second, ask each child to simply rest on the floor and wiggle like a worm, stretching and contracting, incorporating a little creative dramatics. Third, use the relay as a total team effort. Ask the first child in line to run to the opposite end of the room and back.

This time, have him form a train with the person next in line and run down the floor and back, each time, adding the next player until all members are linked. The winning team is the team that "stays together."

5. **Apple Toss**—Play this game similar to an egg toss. Have each child choose a partner. Give each couple an apple. As they face each other, they gently toss the apple to their partner. If he catches it, they each take one step backwards. The team which is the farthest apart and has not dropped the apple wins.

14

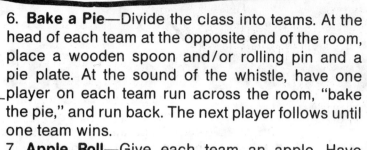

6. **Bake a Pie**—Divide the class into teams. At the head of each team at the opposite end of the room, place a wooden spoon and/or rolling pin and a pie plate. At the sound of the whistle, have one player on each team run across the room, "bake the pie," and run back. The next player follows until one team wins.

7. **Apple Roll**—Give each team an apple. Have players roll the apple across the room with their noses. Ask children to run back with the apple and let the next student try.

8. **Pick a Peck**—Use the basket and apples suggested in activity #3. At the far end of the room place the basket filled with several apples. The first child in line must run to the basket and carry it (with apples) back to the next player in line. Ask this child to return the basket to the opposite end of the room and carefully empty the basket. He then returns empty-handed. The next player must then fill the basket and run back with it. (One player fills the basket; the next one empties it.)

9. **Bob for Apples**—Here's some old-fashioned fun! Place a large tub filled with water and several apples at the opposite end of the room. The first player must run down to the tub, get an apple in his mouth without using his hands, and then run back with the apple to the end of his line. Play continues until one team has all players with an apple.

10. **Apple Hop**—Give the first person on each team an apple. Have him place the apple between his thighs and hop to the far end of the room. He then must carry the apple back to the next player in line who repeats the activity.

11. **"A Peel"ing to Me**—Use this activity with caution, perhaps with older children at camp. Give each person an apple and a potato peeler. As a contest, see which child can cut the longest peeling from his apple.

15

GA1146

Incredible Edibles

Fun with Food?
Party Favors?
A Class Contest?

Your students are sure to enjoy these Incredible Edibles, especially if they can create them!

Place several foods on the table. Give each child an apple. Have him create an apple using toothpicks and the foods provided.

Allow the student to experiment by using foods cut in different ways. Color can also be discussed as projects evolve.

Display finished projects for other children to view.

You may wish to guide younger children as they strive to complete a particular form.

Provide time for older children to develop their own patterns/forms.

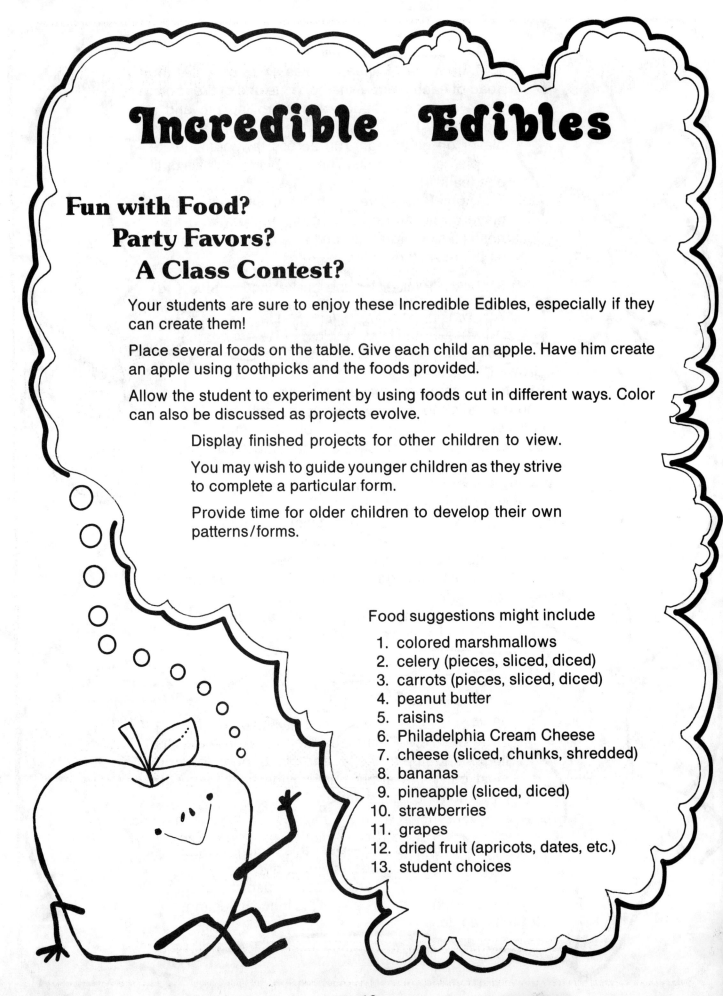

Food suggestions might include

1. colored marshmallows
2. celery (pieces, sliced, diced)
3. carrots (pieces, sliced, diced)
4. peanut butter
5. raisins
6. Philadelphia Cream Cheese
7. cheese (sliced, chunks, shredded)
8. bananas
9. pineapple (sliced, diced)
10. strawberries
11. grapes
12. dried fruit (apricots, dates, etc.)
13. student choices

GA1146

POETRY in MOTION

Finger Play

I was walking in my yard (step in place)
And what should I see? (hold hand to forehead)
A big, juicy apple (make apple shape in air)
Growing on a tree!
Along came the wind (make blowing sound)
And blew it to the ground.
I wanted a bite
So I looked all around. (turn head from left to right)
I looked at that apple,
So shiny and bright,
My mouth opened wide
And I took a bite! (pretend to eat apple)
Apple juice started
To run down my chin. (wipe chin on sleeve)
Then I noticed a little worm (use hand to show how small)
Wiggle back in. (wiggle)
My appetite left! (rub tummy)
I'd had my fill! (nod head yes)
I rolled that big apple
Right down the hill. (roll apple away)

The poem is organized as a finger play, complete with motions. It can be readily adapted to a presentation using full-size poster paper covered with red foil accented with green foil leaves. What a creative feature to use in an Apple Blossom Festival!

GA1146

Appealing to Me

Use oaktag to make the apple and worm patterns for your writing center. On the following page you will find numerous ideas to encourage your students to write. Be sure to add ideas of your own, or even suggestions from your children.

(CUT line between dots)

18

GA1146

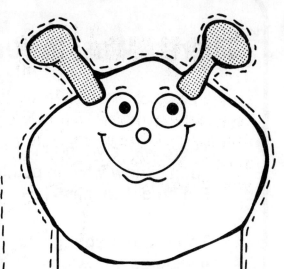

Create a recipe for something or someone—friend, food, month, school.

Write a story about your favorite apple treat.

Pretend you are Johnny Appleseed. Describe your adventures.

Write a report about apples to present to your class.

Read a book about apples and write a summary of it to share.

Design an apple toy. Write an advertisement to "sell" your toy.

Write a story about an apple and give it to a friend to complete.

Make a list of all the apple dishes, treats, recipes you know.

Write directions for making an apple pie. Use words like *first, then*, etc.

Use a dictionary to compile a list of apple words or phrases.

Pretend that you are an apple. Write a story about your life.

Create a poem about an apple.

Write a song about an apple to teach your class.

Write a letter requesting information about apples.

With a friend create a play about apples. Present it to the class.

Display an apple cartoon in the classroom.

GA1146

There Was a Young Man Who Planted a Seed
(Choral Reading)

There was a young man who planted a seed.
I don't know why he planted a seed.
But he did. Indeed!

There was a young man whose seed did sprout.
It wiggled and wiggled until it popped out.
To make it grow he watered the seed.
I don't know why he planted a seed.
But he did. Indeed!

There was a young man whose plant did leaf.
How brief! That little leaf!
His plant did leaf and continue to sprout.
It wiggled and wiggled until it popped out.
To make it grow he watered the seed.
I don't know why he planted a seed.
But he did. Indeed!

There was a young man whose plant grew tall.
In summer, spring, fall it grew tall.
His plant grew tall and continued to leaf.
How brief! That little leaf!
His plant did leaf and continue to sprout.
It wiggled and wiggled until it popped out.
To make it grow he watered the seed.
I don't know why he planted a seed.
But he did. Indeed!

GA1146

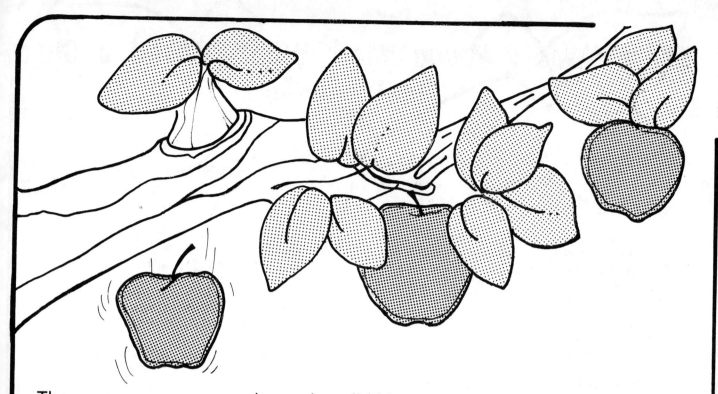

There was a young man whose plant did blossom.
How awesome, that pretty white blossom!
His plant grew bushy and very tall.
In summer, spring, fall it grew tall.
His plant grew tall and continued to leaf.
How brief! That little leaf!
His plant did leaf and continue to sprout.
It wiggled and wiggled until it popped out.
To make it grow he watered the seed.
I don't know why he planted a seed.
But he did. Indeed!

There was a young man whose flowers made fruit.
How cute! Green, yellow, red fruit.
His plant was covered all over with blossom.
How awesome, that pretty white blossom!
His plant grew bushy and very tall.
In summer, spring, fall it grew tall.
His plant grew tall and continued to leaf.
How brief! That little leaf!
His plant did leaf and continue to sprout.
It wiggled and wiggled until it popped out.
To make it grow he watered the seed.
I don't know why he planted a seed.
But he did. Indeed!

There was a young man who ate of this tree.
He's here, you see!

21

GA1146

Props

1. A student dressed like Johnny Apple-seed who will go through the motions of the poem as it is recited.
2. A student dressed in green to be the sprout or a child holding a poster of a sprout.
3. A student dressed in green with leaves attached to his body or a drawing of plant with leaf.
4. A student dressed in green to be a tall plant or a child holding a poster of a tall plant with developing leaves.
5. A student dressed in brown (trunk) and green (treetop) with blossoms attached or a poster of a blossoming apple tree.
6. Students dressed as complete trees bearing red, green, and yellow apples; or posters of apples on trees; or several students holding huge different colored apples.
7. A large apple for Johnny to eat at the end of the reading.

Notes

1. Assign students not in the presentation to read the poem for the audience.
2. Teach the class a song about Johnny Appleseed to sing following the program.
3. Choose a way to present this story which best suits the needs of your class.
4. Add background scenery if you like.
5. Challenge your students to add ideas of their own.

Comments

GA114

APPLE FESTIVAL TIME

Take time to celebrate with your class this fall or next spring. Highlight the festival by selecting favorite activities from the list below. Involve your students as well as staff and parents to plan an exciting day.

1. Invite these people participating to prepare their favorite apple recipes to serve the guests. Ask them to bring serving utensils.
2. Decorate your bulletin board with apple characters, recipes.
3. Display apple art projects around your classroom.
4. Create some Incredible Edibles (see page 16) with your class to use as centerpieces for the refreshment table.
5. Practice the choral reading (see pages 20-21) and present it to those attending the festival.
6. Design apple dolls to use as decorations or favors.
7. Teach your children the finger play (see page 17) to perform at the festival.
8. Involve your students in the Fun Fruit Relays (see page 14). Invite another class to participate with you. Divide students into teams for competition.
9. Make each child a large red, green or yellow poster board apple to carry in an apple parade. Choreograph a simple dance for students to perform as they move around the parade route.
10. Select a song to teach your class about apples. You may want the song to accompany a dance.
11. Read a story about Johnny Appleseed. September 26 is his special day, perhaps the day you want to schedule this festival.
12. Invite adults to make homemade apple butter outside your classroom.
13. Show a filmstrip/movie about apples.
14. Display several books about apples.

GA1146

24

GA1146

GET IT TOGETHER

A pencil box just in time for fall! Color a story, draw a conclusion, toss in a sticky situation, cut out a neat story idea, and see how your writing skills measure up! Your children will be excited about this special creative writing center.

25

GA1146

MY PENCIL BOX
Writing Center

This creative writing center is sure to delight your students. Set up a display in a quiet spot in your room where children can work independently on the station activities after instructions from you.

The envelope on the following page will provide an efficient way to keep track of each child's progress. As he completes a section of the station, have him insert his work into the envelope. You will need to determine, specifically, your method of grading and the length of time you wish to designate for completing this station. There are five different types of writing assignments. Slight teacher preparation is required if you use these ideas as a station. Attach the large "supplies" to the bulletin board on which the story suggestions are given. In a small envelope below each object, place the corresponding shape patterns children will use to complete the particular assignment. Alter the activities to satisfy the needs of your classroom.

Once the station is ready, decide whether you want children to be scheduled through the activities or to work freely to complete story assignments.

GA114

My Pencil Box

My Pencil Box writing center is a fun approach to creative writing. The organization is quite simple! Give each child a large envelope and a copy of the picture below. Have him glue the picture to the front of the envelope. This will be his "pencil box" in which he will store all of his writing assignments. Ask him to write his name on the envelope as well as each activity he inserts in his "pencil box." When the station is completed, each child will have glue, scissors, pencil, crayons and a ruler in his envelope for you to grade.

GA1146

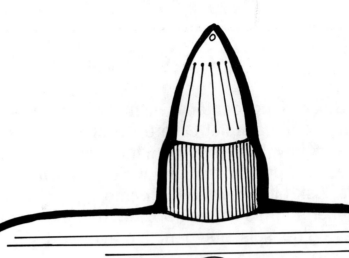

Sticky Situations

Select one topic. Write a paragraph about it on the glue bottle pattern.

1. You have two best friends who both want you to themselves.

2. You and your sister/brother share a bedroom. You are neat and he/she is messy.

3. For the summer you have gotten a job. After a week on the job, you realize it's not for you. You need the money.

4. You have a very popular best friend. How do you handle all the attention he/she gets?

5. You seem to have a lot of homework this year. It's difficult to get it finished because it is very noisy at home and you have several chores to do each day.

6. You want to get involved in school clubs and activities. You live far from the school and your parents both work.

GA114

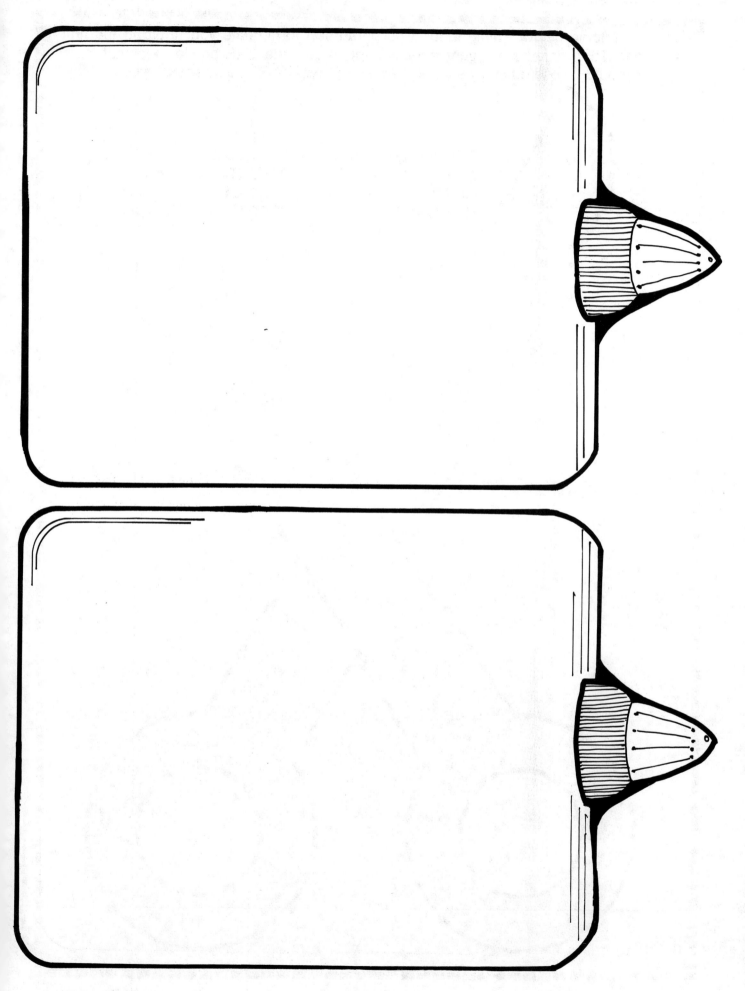

29

Choose a topic below. Think about it! In paragraph form, state your topic in the first sentence. Then state several sentences to support your ideas. (Example: I feel that more sports should be offered at my school.) Write your response on a scissors card.

RECESS   FRIENDS
SCHOOL LUNCHES TEACHERS
SCHOOL RULES   PARENTS
CLUBS   CLASSES
HOMEWORK   SPORTS

"CUT" SESSION

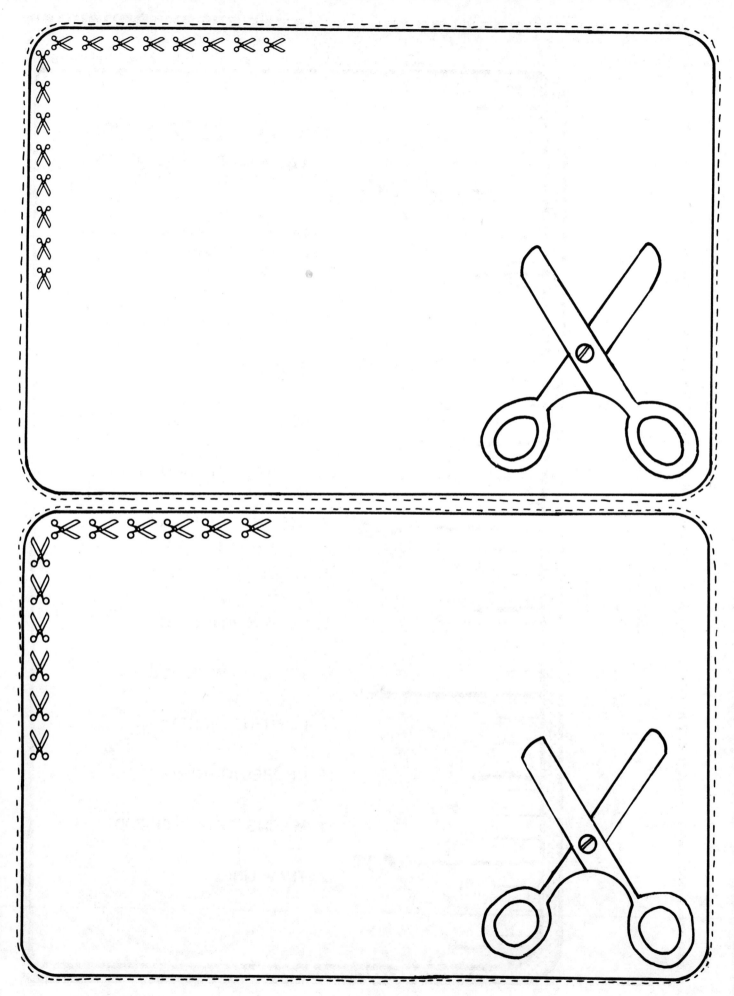

31

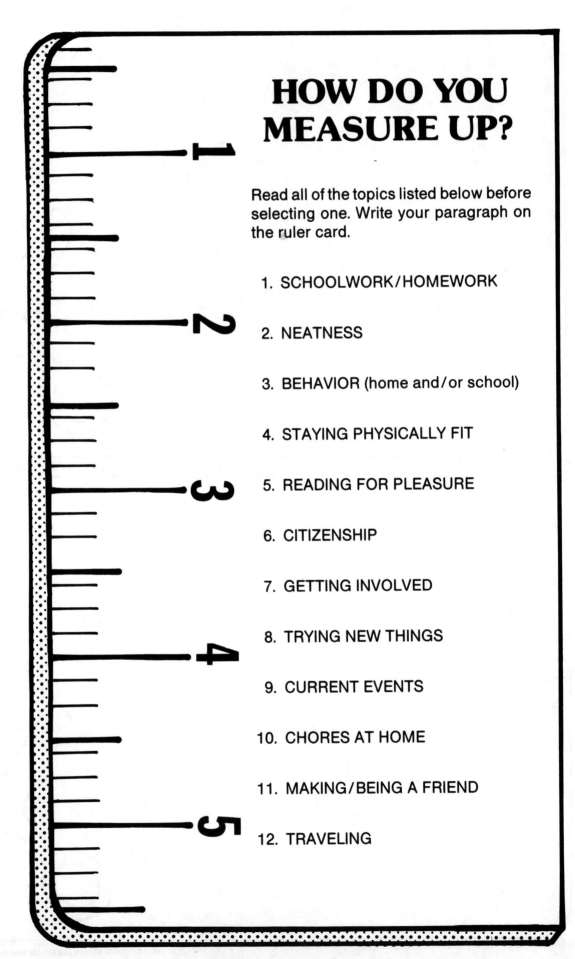

HOW DO YOU MEASURE UP?

Read all of the topics listed below before selecting one. Write your paragraph on the ruler card.

1. SCHOOLWORK/HOMEWORK

2. NEATNESS

3. BEHAVIOR (home and/or school)

4. STAYING PHYSICALLY FIT

5. READING FOR PLEASURE

6. CITIZENSHIP

7. GETTING INVOLVED

8. TRYING NEW THINGS

9. CURRENT EVENTS

10. CHORES AT HOME

11. MAKING/BEING A FRIEND

12. TRAVELING

GA1146

33

Colorful Writing

Good authors use verbs, adjectives, and adverbs to describe people, places, and things in their stories. These words help the writer "picture" the scene. Select a topic below. Write it in big letters on the back of your crayon pattern. Then list several words that describe your topic. On the front of your crayon pattern, use some of your words in a paragraph to describe your topic.

FAVORITE FOOD
MY PET
FAVORITE SPORT
MY SCHOOL

BEST VACATION
FAVORITE CHARACTER
TV SHOW
FUNNIEST MEMORY
AUTUMN
HAUNTED HOUSE
BEST FRIEND
MY FAMILY
PARK
HOBBY
FAMILY MEMBER
FAVORITE PLACE
BEST BOOK
BICYCLE

GA1146

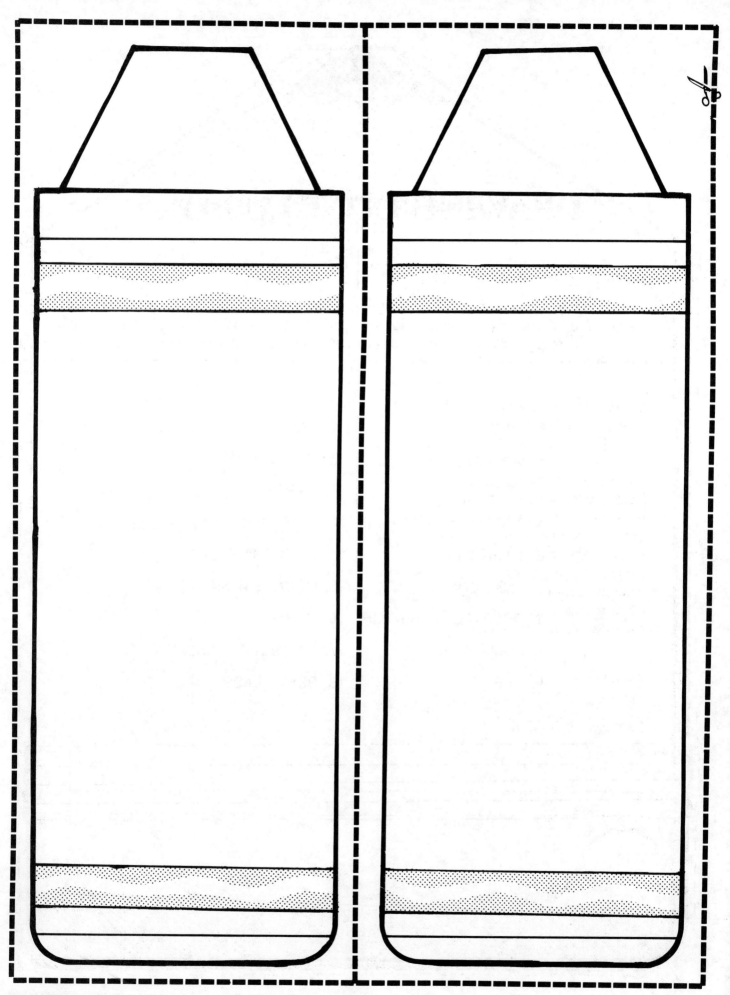

35

GA1146

DRAWING CONCLUSIONS

Have yourself a little fun. Read through the list of topics below. Choose one or use an idea of your own. Take a survey. Use the back of your pencil pattern to record your data. Then on the front of the pencil pattern, "draw" your conclusions using pictures.

1. FOOD
2. SPORTS
3. PETS
4. PEOPLE IN THE NEWS
5. TV SHOW
6. FASHIONS
7. GREATEST INVENTOR
8. SUMMER JOB
9. HERO

10. HOBBY
11. VIDEO GAMES
12. CAREERS
13. MUSEUMS
14. CURRENT EVENT
15. GREATEST MOVIE
16. CARS
17. FAVORITE SEASON
18. BEST CLASS

GA1146

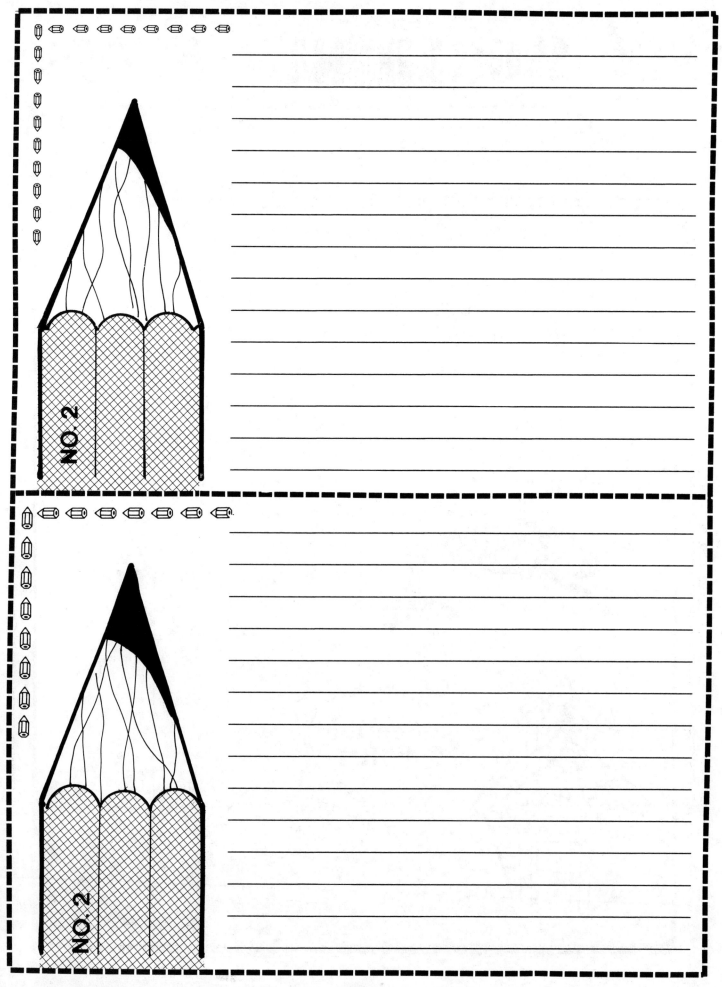

GA1146

SEE WORLD BUS STOPS

See the
SCHOOL

Acquaint your students with their school by taking them on field trips in and around the school location.

Give students a copy of this school booklet. Have them color it, cut it out, and staple it at the top.

Spend the remaining four days completing the booklet, one page per day. Your children will become comfortable in their new surroundings as you familiarize them with their school and its many facets.

MY SCHOOL

39

GA1146

Exit the front doors of your school. Take a field trip around your school grounds. Bring this booklet and a pencil with you. Write answers to the following questions.

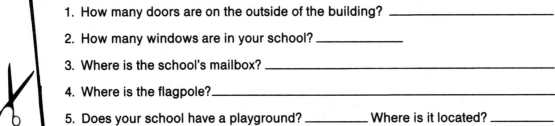

OUTSIDE MY SCHOOL

1. How many doors are on the outside of the building? _____

2. How many windows are in your school? _____

3. Where is the school's mailbox? _____

4. Where is the flagpole? _____

5. Does your school have a playground? _____ Where is it located? _____
_____

6. Name the equipment found on the playground. _____
_____
_____

7. What is the land like around your school? _____
_____

8. What type of plants are on the school grounds? _____
_____

9. Where is the name of the school written? _____

10. Where do the teachers park their vehicles? _____

11. How many parking lots are there? _____

GA1146

Carry this booklet and your pencil with you as you explore inside your school. Remember to walk quietly so you won't disturb others. Can you answer the questions below?

INSIDE MY SCHOOL

1. How many rooms are in the school? _____

2. How many steps are there from your chair to the principal's office? _____

3. There are _____ cooks in the school.

4. How many bathrooms are in your school? _____

5. How many water fountains? _____

6. What room in the school is closest to yours? _____

7. How many rooms in the school do you visit on Mondays? _____

8. Which room in the school is your favorite? _____

Why? _____

9. Name ten objects you can find in the principal's office. _____

_____

10. How many teachers work at your school? _____

11. Which teacher teaches nearest you? _____

12. Where are the telephones? _____

13. What is the school's phone number? _____

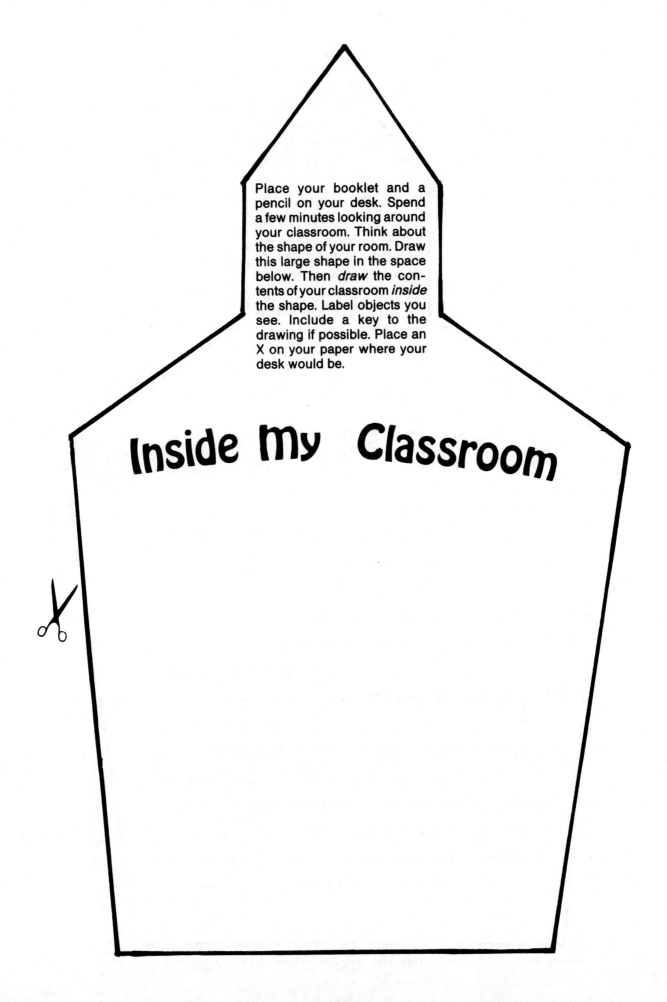

Place your booklet and a pencil on your desk. Spend a few minutes looking around your classroom. Think about the shape of your room. Draw this large shape in the space below. Then *draw* the contents of your classroom *inside* the shape. Label objects you see. Include a key to the drawing if possible. Place an X on your paper where your desk would be.

Inside My Classroom

GA1146

Take a field trip inside yourself. Take this booklet and a pencil and find a quiet spot to work. Think for a few minutes about yourself. See if you can answer the questions below.

INSIDE MYSELF

1. When I have free time I like to _____
   _____

2. One of my favorite family members is _____ because _____
   _____

3. Whenever I have a problem I talk to _____

4. My best friend is _____. Three things I admire about
   this person are _____

5. The best thing I like about myself is_____

6. If I could change anything about myself it would be _____
   _____

7. If I were an animal, I'd choose to be a _____ because
   _____

8. I would like to be _____ years old because _____
   _____

9. The person I admire most is _____ because _____
   _____

10. I have a dream that someday I _____

11. If I were rich, I'd _____

12. Sometimes I get mad when_____
    When I am mad I _____

13. Things that make me happiest are_____
    _____

See the
FARM

44

SEE THE FARM

To locate information on the map, you will need to use a letter and a number to identify the exact spot where something is. Always state the letter first and then the number.

1. What animal do you see in B1? _____

2. There are _____ ladybugs in B6.

3. In E4 you will find a _____

4. The pig is in _____.

5. Draw a baby lamb in F4.

6. In E2 draw three carrots. Color them.

7. There are _____ in F6.

8. Draw a farmer in B4 and B5. Color him.

9. The cow's head is in _____.

10. In A1 draw a small turtle.

11. In _____ you will find the horse's head.

12. The horse's tail is in _____.

13. Draw a small cat in A4.

14. In B3 you will find _____.

15. The barn covers these squares: _____

_____

GA1146

See the AQUARIUM

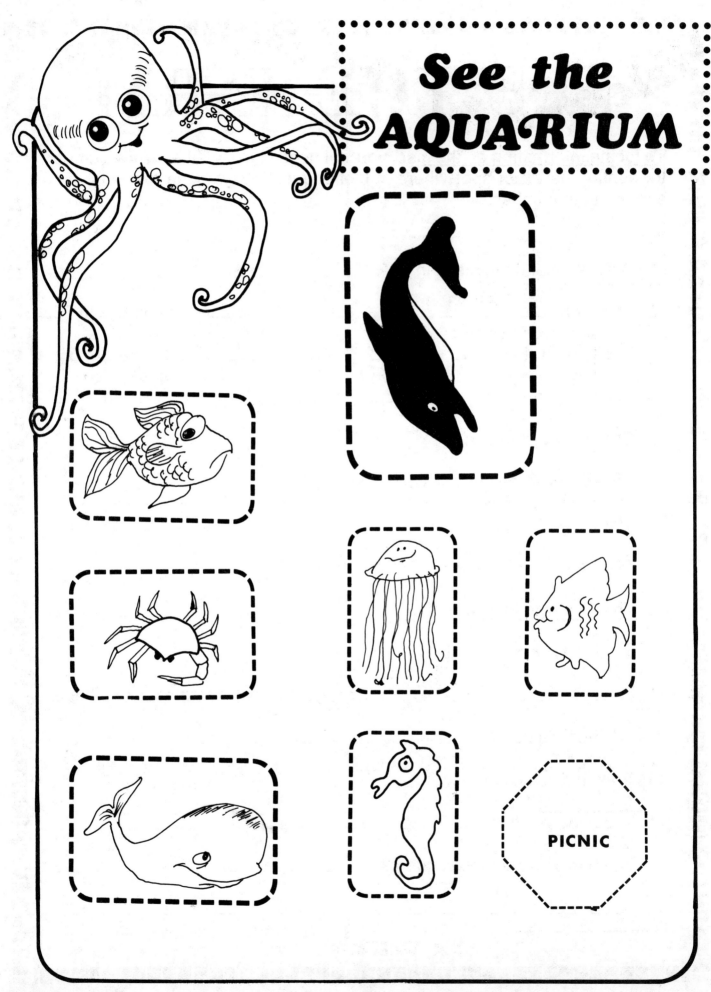

PICNIC

46

GA1146

Welcome to the Aquarium

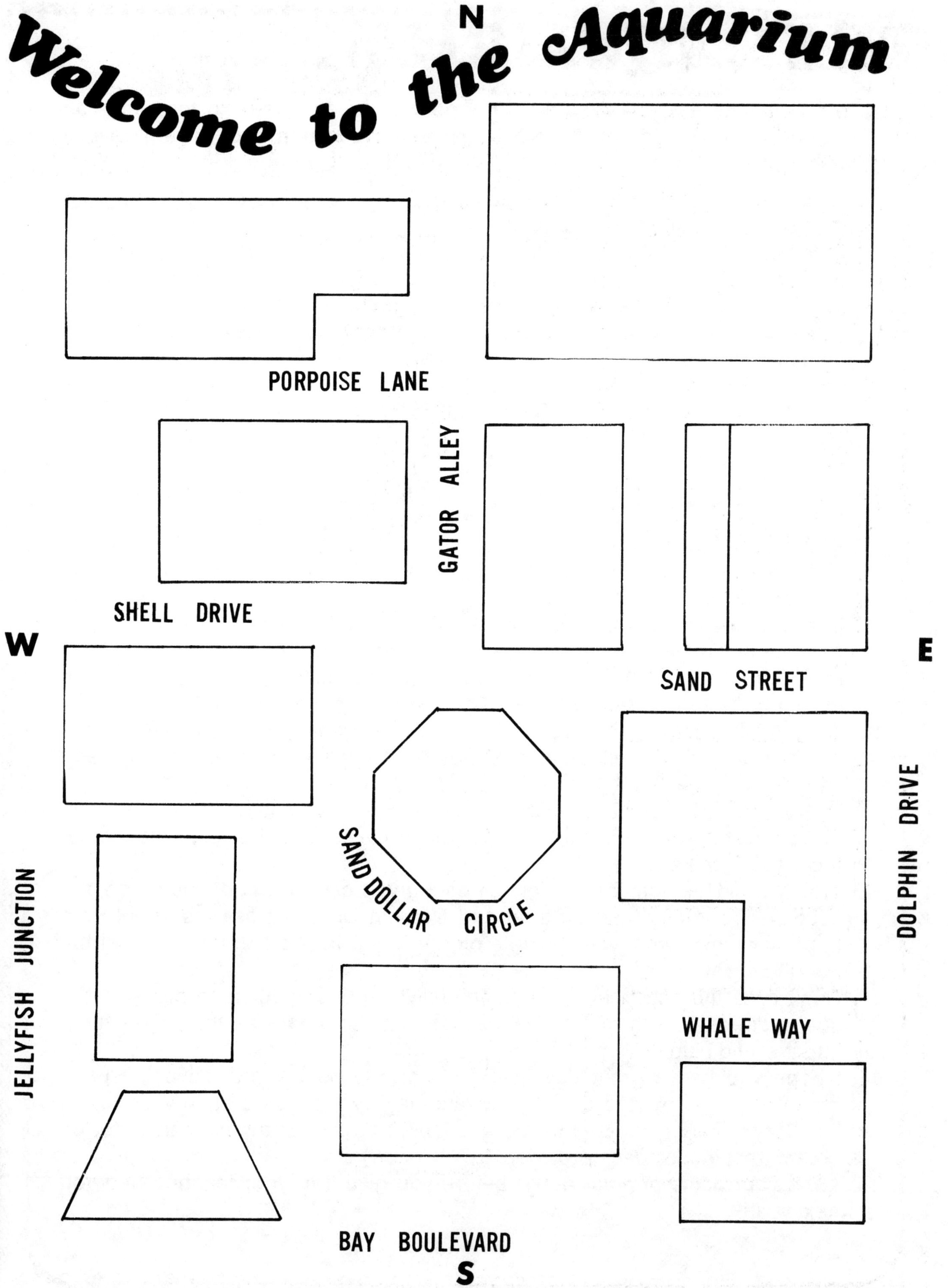

PORPOISE LANE

GATOR ALLEY

SHELL DRIVE

W

SAND STREET

E

DOLPHIN DRIVE

JELLYFISH JUNCTION

SAND DOLLAR CIRCLE

WHALE WAY

BAY BOULEVARD

GA1146

THE AQUARIUM

Hello and welcome to the Aquarium. I hope you wil enjoy seeing the sights as you spend a day in one of the most fascinating vacation spots ever! Have a nice day.

1. Color and cut out all of your map pieces from page 46 and glue them to the appropriate spaces on page 47.
2. Enter the park from Bay Boulevard and Dolphin Drive. Buy your tickets at the corner office. Draw yourself standing at the Ticket Office. Label the building.
3. The building on the left of the Ticket Office is the Wonderful Whale Pavilion. Glue the correct map piece here. After the show, exit from the rear of the building onto Sand Dollar Circle.
4. Stop for lunch. Enjoy a rest at the Picnic area. Glue your map piece here.
5. On the northeast corner of Gator Alley and Sand Street, you will find the Sea Horse Diving Arena. Glue your map piece here. You'll be thrilled with the marvelous stunts you will see.
6. Time for a bathroom break. Bathrooms are located in the narrow building to the right of Sea Horse Diving Arena. Label the Bathrooms.
7. In the same building as the bathrooms, you will find the largest Fish Tank in the world. Glue your Fish Tank map piece here. Look at all those unique looking fish!
8. In the northeast corner of the park is the Porpoise Pavilion. Glue the map piece here. Sit back and enjoy the show. Watch out for those wet splashes!
9. Don't forget to visit Seaside Souvenirs. It is the building on the left side of the Porpoise Pavilion. Draw your favorite souvenirs here. Color them.
10. Claim your prize for the biggest catch at the Fishing Hole, located on the northwest side of Shell Drive and Gator Alley. Glue your map piece here. How big was that fish?
11. By now your stomach is probably growling. You have two choices for dinner. The closest to you is the Crab House, just to the south of Fishing Hole. Attach the map piece here.
12. The second choice for dinner is the Food Festival Court, found on the southwest corner of Sand Street and Dolphin Drive, across the street from the bathrooms. Draw your favorite dinner menu inside the space. Label the Food Festival Court.
13. Don't miss the action at the Jumpin' Jellyfish. Glue your map piece to the space directly south of Crab House. Hold your breath as the skiers jump into the wild blue!
14. I hope you had a great day at the Aquarium. Before you leave the park, be sure to stop by and select your favorite flavor of ice cream. Visit Josh's Ice Cream Parlor, located in the southwest corner. Draw your favorite ice cream treat in the space provided.
15. Write your name on your paper before you give it to your teacher. See you next year!

GA1146

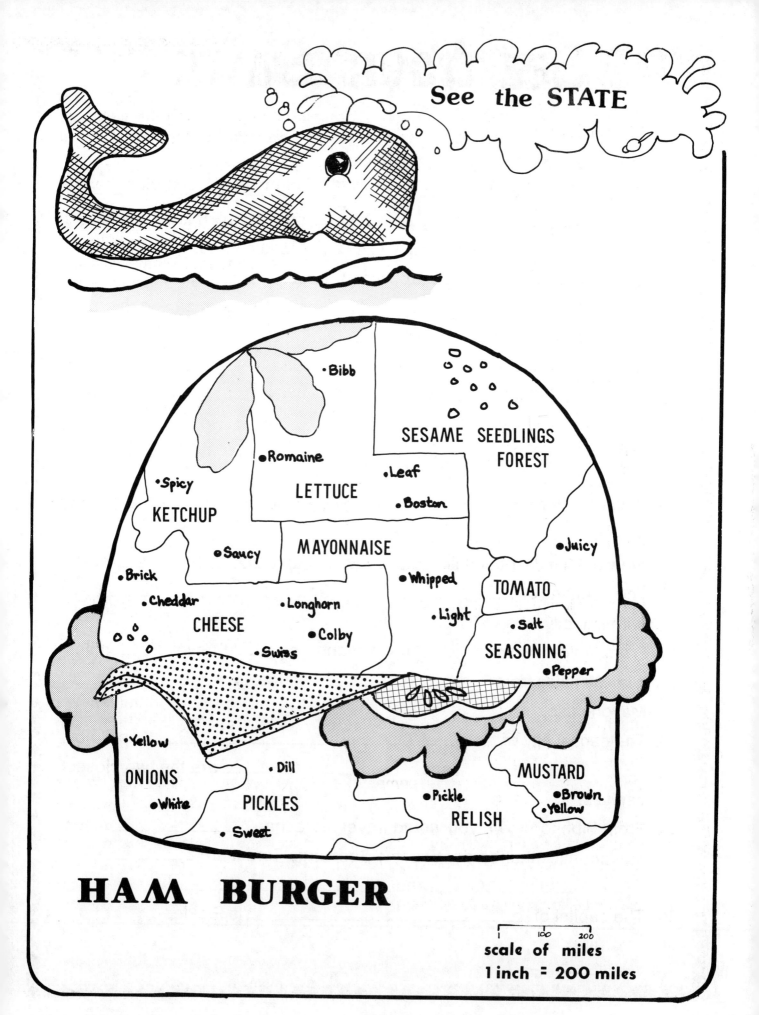

See the STATE

SESAME SEEDLINGS FOREST

• Bibb

• Romaine

• Spicy

LETTUCE

• Leaf

• Boston

KETCHUP

• Saucy

MAYONNAISE

• Juicy

• Brick

• Whipped

TOMATO

• Cheddar

• Longhorn

• Light

• Salt

CHEESE

• Colby

SEASONING

• Swiss

• Pepper

• Yellow

• Dill

MUSTARD

ONIONS

• Pickle

• Brown

• White

PICKLES

RELISH

• Yellow

• Sweet

HAM BURGER

scale of miles

100   200

1 inch = 200 miles

49

GA1146

See Your State

1. The name of the state is _____

2. The state is divided into ten counties: _____ , _____ ,
   _____ , _____ , _____ ,
   _____ , _____ , _____ ,

3. _____ is a forest in Ham Burger.

4. What town is listed on the map twice? _____

5. _____ is the most southern city on the map.

6. The county with the most cities is _____

7. Saucy and Spicy are approximately _____ miles apart.

8. To go from Brick to Pickle you would travel about _____ miles.

9. In Cheese, it is about 300 miles from _____ to _____ .

10. From Cheddar, Cheese, to Juicy, Tomato, you would travel approximately
    _____ miles.

11. It is 600 miles from _____ , Pickles, to _____ ,
    Mustard.

12. From Bibb to Pepper it is _____ miles.

13. The counties of _____ and _____ have
    only one city.

14. From Yellow, Mustard, to Yellow, Onions, you would travel _____ miles.

15. It is 400 miles from _____ , Lettuce, to _____ ,
    Mayonnaise.

16. The capital city of _____ is Colby.

17. _____ and _____ are the two closest
    capitals.

18. From Bibb to Brown you would travel more than _____ miles.

19. The counties that border Sesame Seedlings Forest are _____ ,
    _____ and _____ .

20. The capital of _____ is Pickle.

50

rain
shine
spring
fall
MOTIVATORS
help
us
all

Welcome Rally

51

Materials:
  Yellow paper for background
  Large white cloud with black lettering
  Large red apple with green leaf, brown stem, black and white eyes
  Library card pocket for each child
  Oaktag on which to print monthly pattern and incentive card for each
    child (see page 55 for specific patterns)
  Markers or crayons for decorating oaktag patterns
  Glue for assembling monthly motivators

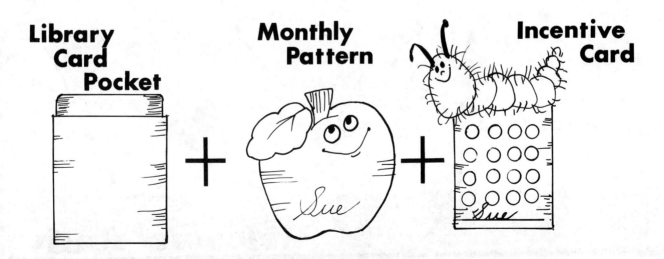

Library
Card
Pocket
  +
Monthly
Pattern
  +
Incentive
Card

GA1146

Directions:

1. Place the yellow background paper on the bulletin board.

2. Attach the cloud with lettering and the large red apple with decorated features to the bulletin board.

3. Give each child a Library Card Pocket.

4. Xerox an oaktag monthly pattern and incentive card for each student. Ask him to decorate them, cut them out, and write his name on both patterns.

5. Demonstrate to the class how to glue the monthly pattern to the front of the Library Card Pocket, being careful to show that sometimes the pattern will be bigger than the card so it may hang over. Remind children **not** to glue the pocket closed.

6. Show children how to slide the decorated incentive chart into the pocket. Do not have them glue it in!

7. Attach the completed motivators to the bulletin board.

8. Explain to the class your purpose for using the monthly motivators. (See ideas on the next page.)

9. Be sure to mention to the children that only you will be punching the cards or placing stickers on the little circles. Tell children that as rows of circles are covered with stickers or punched out, you will expose that part of their card as it is raised from the library card pocket on the bulletin board.

10. Explain to the children when they may take their cards home. You may want them to be sent home with the children, mailed home, placed in the envelope with the report card, or kept for parent-teacher conferences.

11. Tell the children what, if any, reward they will receive at the end of the month or specified time period. The punched card/pocket may be all that is necessary. Perhaps a little treat or extra play time is essential. You need to determine this ahead of time so that children will know your intentions. Verbal, positive reinforcement in the presence of the entire class may be the goal toward which you'll strive.

GA1146

USE MONTHLY MOTIVATORS...

- To record completed homework assignments.

- To reinforce good behavior. To reinforce specific behavior, such as staying in seats, raising hands before speaking, being prepared for class, keeping a neat desk.

- To honor students who make 100 percent on tests. These grades could be received in all classes or perhaps a specific class, such as spelling.

- To record the number of books a student reads during the month. These could be verified by you as the children read books at school. Parents could write a note verifying that their child has read a book at home.

- To provide an incentive for book reports: oral, written, other.

- To show attendance for the month.

- To brag on good deeds/citizenship/sportsmanship performed in the classroom or around the school.

- To inspire children to complete classwork during class time.

- To encourage children to complete chores in the classroom, such as washing boards, stacking chairs, cleaning the floor.

- To record completed extra credit projects.

- To show mastery of specific skills: math facts, states and capitals, countries and capitals, reading vocabulary.

GA1146

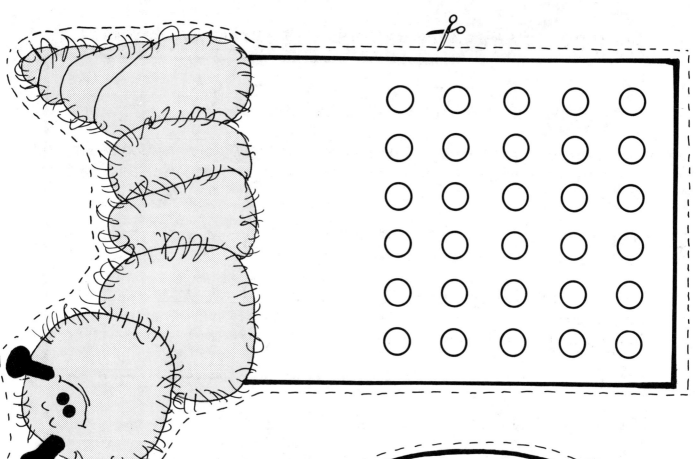

September
GOOD APPLES Pattern

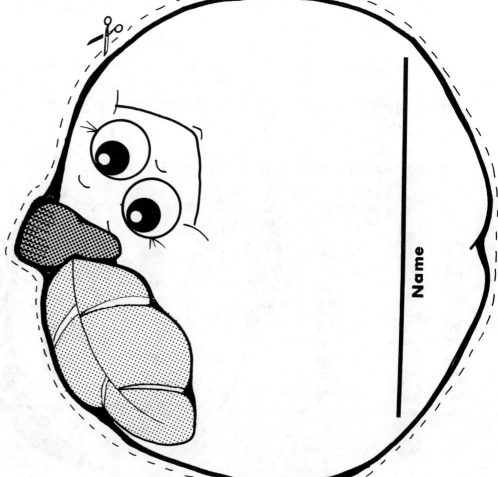

Name

55

GA1146

October
SPECTACULAR SPOOKS
Pattern

Name

GA1146

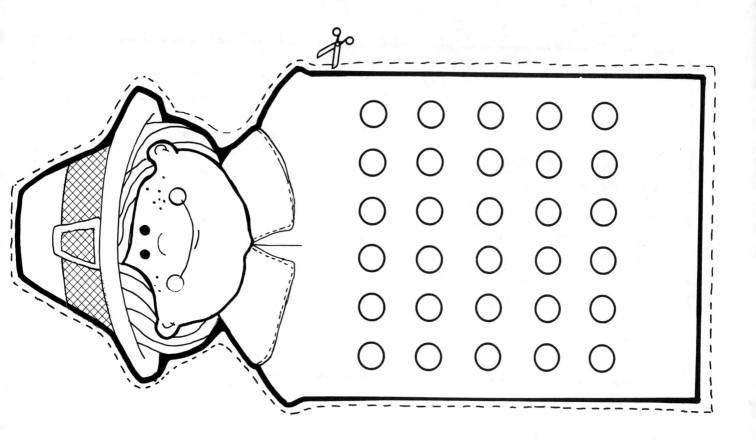

November
TOP TURKEYS
Pattern

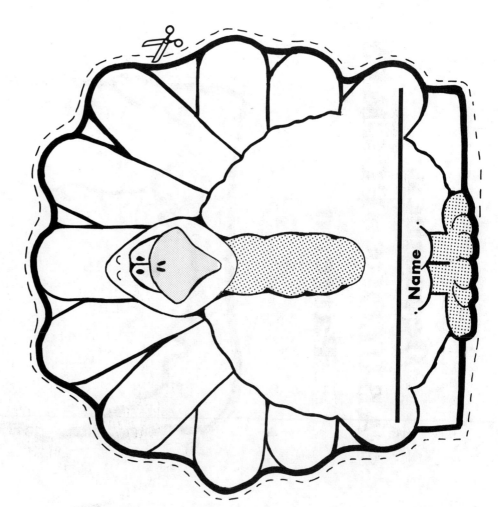

Name

GA1146

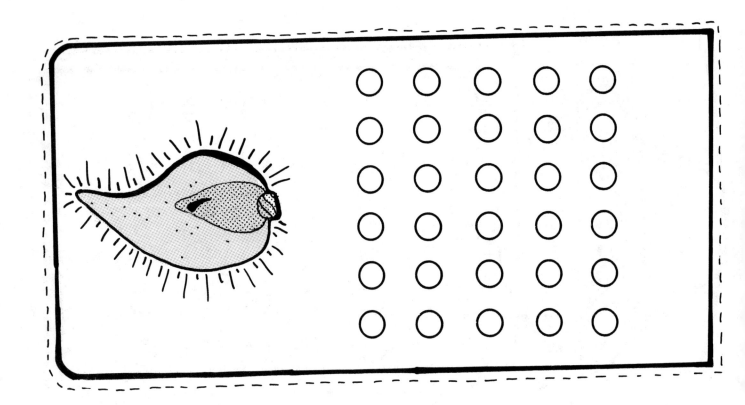

December
FABULOUS FLAMES
Pattern

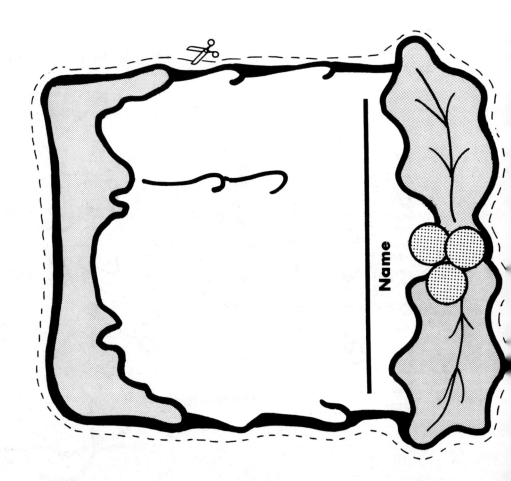

Name

GA1146

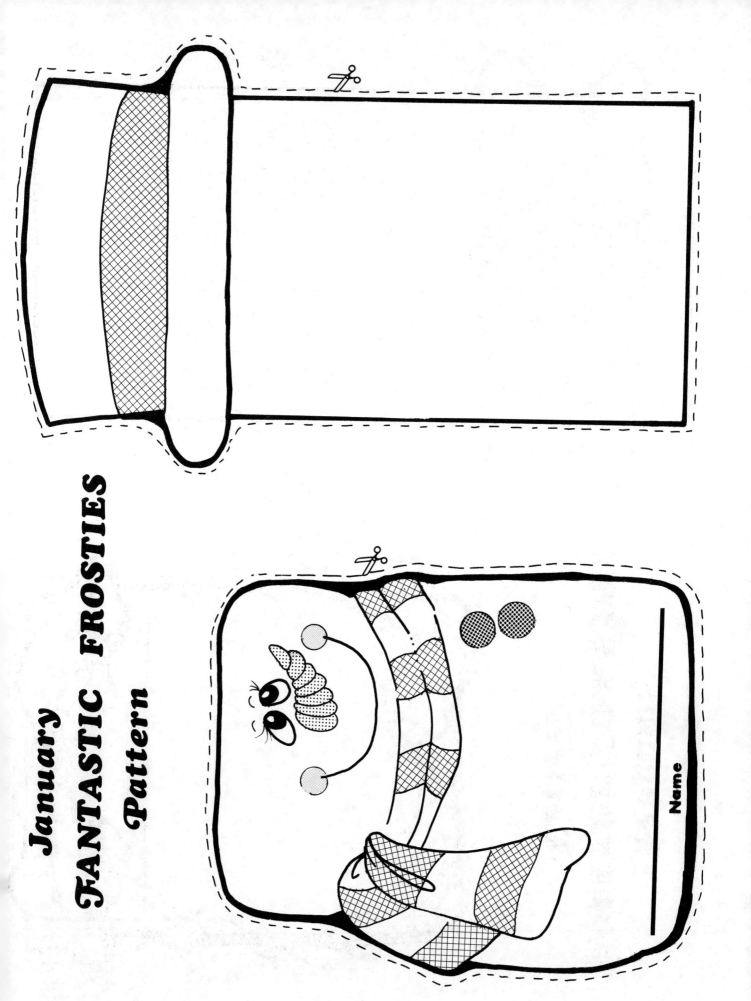

January
FANTASTIC FROSTIES
Pattern

Name

59

GA1146

February
HAPPY HEARTS Pattern

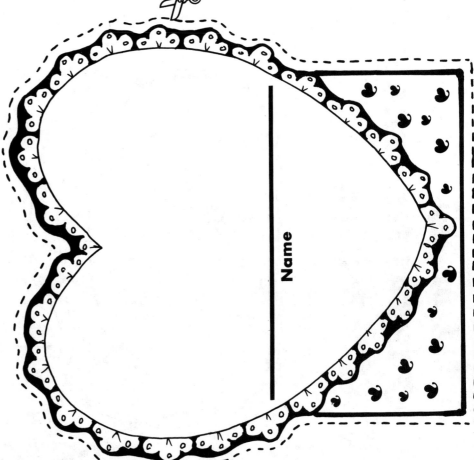

Name

60

March
RESPONSIBLE RABBITS
Pattern

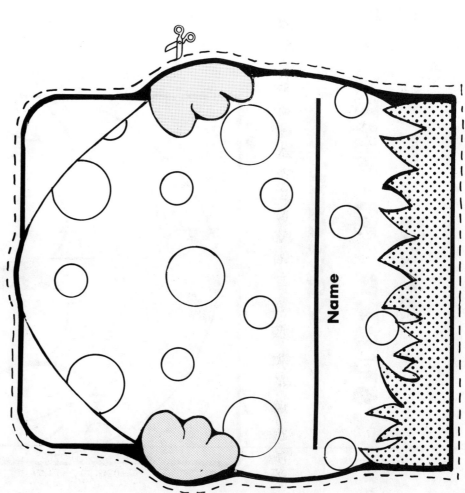

Name

61

GA1146

April
SUPER SUNBEAMS
Pattern

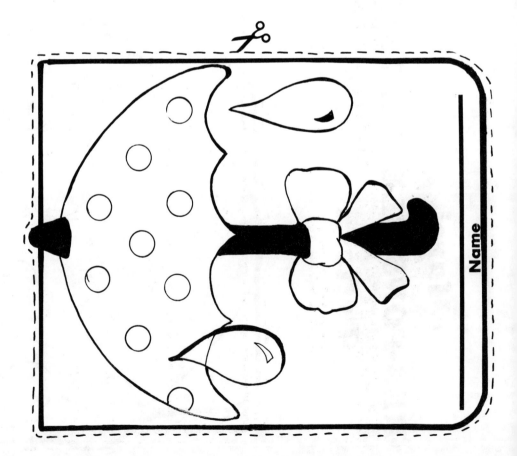

Name

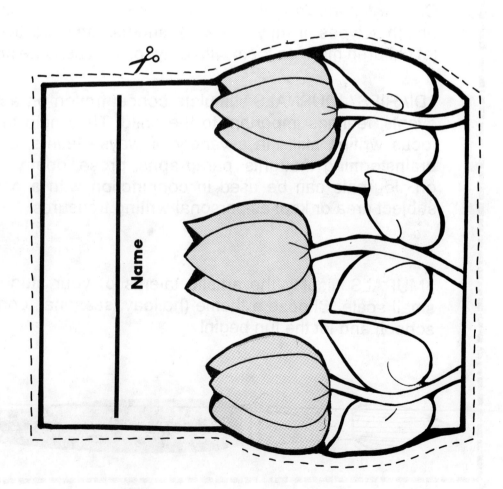

May

BLOSSOMING BEAUTIES

Pattern

Name

63

GA1146

DAY-to-DAY MOTIVATORS

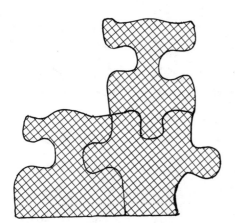

Ongoing activities provide stability in your teaching schedule. They challenge, they interest, and they provide a change of pace in everyday situations. They promote individual independence as well as team or class cooperation. They provide motivation and help control discipline problems by encouraging students to make choices during idle time. Read through the ideas presented, and then plug them into your routine whenever possible. Be sure to introduce new ideas in your room to the children and remind them of the care they should give the new materials.

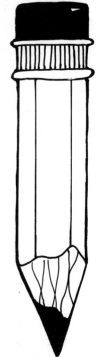

*PUZZLES encourage eye-hand coordination and teamwork. Choose interlocking jigsaws, crosswords, word hunts, rebus or other types. If they are work sheets, laminate them and let children mark on them with crayons or washable markers.

*DIARIES/JOURNALS stimulate concentration on activities, events, feelings important to the child. They help the child focus writing skills in a variety of ways—letters, opinions, brainstorming thoughts, paragraphs, prose, poetry, and so on. Journals can be used in conjunction with a particular subject area or kept as personal writing treasures.

*MURALS display the artistic talents of your students on a large or small scale. Choose a theme (holiday, seasonal, content area, back to school) and let the fun begin!

GA1146

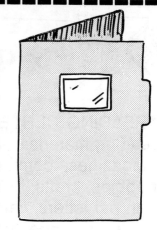

*FILE FOLDERS hold the daily, weekly, or monthly papers of each student. Ask students to decorate their folders and print their names clearly on the tabs. Keep folders in a central place in the room so that corrected papers can be added by you or the children. When papers come home as a group, parents sometimes have a better idea of how their child is progressing over a period of time. File folders are great organizers for parent conferences. No more lost papers in the desk!

*ESTIMATION STATION challenges children to guess height, weight, length, quantity, or other measurements of objects the teacher places at the center. You'll be amazed at how rapidly estimation skills increase. Place pencil and paper at the station for student guesses and be sure to explain or post the station rules before competition begins. Reward the winner.

*ORAL READING relaxes children. Ask your librarian for a list of medal-winning books appropriate to your grade level. Listening skills will be developed as well as a love of reading when you consistently provide a pleasant atmosphere for sharing books. When children return from a trip to the library, take a few minutes to let them discuss the books they have chosen. If your children participate in any paperback book clubs, let them read orally the advertisements to the books when you pass out the order forms. When new books arrive, let students show their new selections. Encourage children to read on their own. Set the example yourself! Read daily!

★READING CENTER

*READING CENTER encourages ALL children to read! Place a variety of reading materials which will attract children to frequent the center: recipes, magazines, comic books, baseball/football cards, books about sports, hobbies, crafts, holidays, topics about which you are studying, pamphlets, pen pal letters, catalogs, student creative writing stories, joke books, short stories. Change materials often to keep children interested.

*ART GALLERY builds confidence in art by attractively displaying children's work throughout the year. Try to expose students to different art media and techniques.

*PEN PALS stimulate interest in letter writing through total class participation. Pen pals also help develop friendships and interests in other parts of the city/country. Keeps children in touch with feelings and attitudes of children their own age.

*BOOK REPORTS inspire children to read books with understanding and verbalize on paper, orally, or by other means, the summary. Book reports encourage other students to want to read.

GA1146

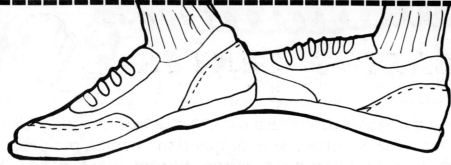

*OLYMPICS/INTRAMURAL SPORTS provide mental and physical competition with other classmates. Sports serve to develop individual as well as team skills. They promote a positive framework for enhancing good citizenship. When organized properly, Olympics challenge the best "athletes," while exposing students to a variety of activities. (Topics for selection might include Math Facts, Top Speller, Best Writer, Most 100's, Fastest Runner, Most Home Runs, Most Goals Scored, etc.)

*CLASS MEETINGS communicate the feelings of both teacher and student through organized oral expression. Directed by the teacher, class meetings should be scheduled at regular intervals. During meetings students should be commended for good behavior/grades, and poor behavior/grades should be reviewed. Involve children in the decision-making process to make them more aware of rules and their consequences when broken. Remember that a positive learning atmosphere, where good citizenship is stressed, is the goal.

*CREATIVE WRITING STATION reinforces writing activities such as prose, poetry, letter writing, handwriting, creative writing, and incorporates skill development in grammar and punctuation.

*CURRENT EVENTS update student understanding or what is happening in the world and where. Encourages children to watch the news and to be able to discuss it with intelligence.

GA1146

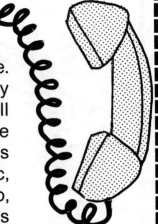

*PHONE CALLS link the school with the home. They provide immediate responses. Try rewarding children with a "good" phone call home or to their parents' workplace. Positive results are overwhelming when parents receive firsthand information about academic, physical, or social progress. Remember, too, the call in times of trouble. (When phone calls are not possible, take a moment to brag about the child in a note or postcard to the home.)

*STICKERS/AWARDS praise a child overtly in a positive manner. They help build good self-concepts.

*RESEARCH—teaches children to use a variety of references to locate information about numerous subjects. It encourages the interested student to look beyond the textbook and present his findings to fellow classmates. It provides a wealth of extra credit possibilities to low achievers. Be sure to exhibit projects students complete in a prominent place.

*SIMON SAYS develops good listeners. The teacher should be "Simon" until children become familiar with the game. Play the game between classes to stimulate physical activity.

*GUEST SPEAKERS bring fresh ideas into your room. Be sure to give them information about your class before they arrive, tell them the exact nature of their presentation, confirm the date just before the speaker is due, and remind your students of proper behavior.

GA1146

*"LET ME ENTERTAIN YOU" translates into a fun time for you and your students. Explain to the children that you have been "entertaining" them for awhile, and now it is their turn. Have students think for a moment about something they would like to do for the class, such as

play the piano or another instrument, tell a joke, ask a riddle, draw something, share a skill, teach a lesson. Don't force hesitant children to perform. They may build up confidence for the next time!

*FIELD TRIPS utilize resources to extend the learning atmosphere. Incorporate parents to accompany you and share in the excitement of the children.

*PEER TUTORING builds confidence in skills learned and encourages relationships in the classroom. Children can be paired with someone on their level or at the other extreme. Older children also relish teaching students in other areas of the school.

*LUNCH WITH THE TEACHER enables both teacher and pupil to view each other in a more personal way. It provides a casual atmosphere to exchange feelings, attitudes.

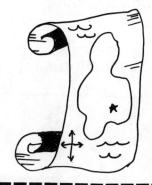

*MAPS/GLOBES provide hands-on experiences in locating old and new places. Expose children to various types and sizes of maps. Ask them to draw and label maps frequently.

GA1146

*SUGGESTION BOX allows students to voice their opinions about topics that directly affect them. It gives the shy student a "speaking" voice.

*DEBATE TEAM promotes teamwork. It encourages research on suggested topics, logical presentation, and the ability to draw conclusions. It widens viewpoints.

*DAILY CHALLENGE sparks a curious mind. The challenge can be in any form: riddle, joke, trivia, current event, new word, contest, problem. Reward the winner in an appropriate way.

*CAMERA captures invaluable moments. Photographs can be used in unlimited ways:

1. To focus on good citizens, honor roll students
2. To highlight school events
3. To supplement the school newspaper
4. To create individual birthday posters
5. To organize/schedule learning centers
6. To show changes in students
7. To personalize booklets, cards
8. To honor students for achievements outside of school activities (talents, community involvement)
9. To "share" fun times with other children
10. To provide parents with a tangible, firsthand review of their child in action: playing, working, socializing
11. To create a caper chart
12. To summarize the school year during Open House or graduation (present a slide show titled "A Year in Review")

GA1146

Homework Alternatives...

One of the most troublesome topics discussed by students, teachers, and parents is HOMEWORK! Occasionally substitute a few of these ideas to create a more pleasant and meaningful approach to homework. Give children appropriate time to complete tasks.

* Ask children to interview someone (family member, neighbor, friend). Give the children a specific question, current event, etc., to ask. Remind children of proper etiquette to follow during the interview.

* Give children a gameboard or let them use one of their own. Have students create questions/answers for a particular content area. Also ask them to write down rules for the game. Place rules, game pieces, and game cards in a Baggie. Allow children time to play the game at school. This is a great way to review for a test!

* Plan a "book talk" with your class. Choose a book on their level and begin reading it orally to them. Use lots of expression and enthusiasm. After a few pages or a chapter, stop. Ask children if they would like to read a book to a youngster at home (neighbor/sibling) on a regular basis. Perhaps have the parents sign a paper at home and return it to school when the student has read a book.

* Older children love Show and Tell. Allow them to bring in items related to units you are studying or projects they have made. This is a great motivator for the shy student, as well as a practice in public speaking.

71

GA1146

* "Teacher Time" challenges children to present material they have researched outside the classroom in front of their peers. Ask students to pursue specific areas of study that relate to what you are teaching.

* Ask energetic children to create work sheets to use in conjunction with specific lessons you will teach. Spelling activities—word hunts, scrambled words, fill-in-the-blanks—are simple to create.

* Remind children to bring in newspaper clippings of current events you are discussing. Post them on a bulletin board.

* Encourage children to bring to class large, colored pictures of topics they like. Use the pictures for creative writing topics. Display finished stories by the illustrations.

* Many children are talented and seldom get the chance to perform in front of their class. Invite students to perfect their talents and present them to the children.

* Many children want homework. Keep legal-sized envelopes in your desk. When you have a few extra work sheets, fun sheets, or activities, place them in an envelope for a specific child. This will make it personal. Other children will soon be asking for extra work. Remember! Not all children need the same assignment!

* Have children create a mini calendar (see pages 107-108 for examples). Ask them to share the ideas with classmates to use during a specific month.

* Encourage children to listen to the TV and radio for coming events. At the appropriate time, have them share their news in morning exercises. Ideas might include birthdays of celebrities, dates of inventions, holidays, festivals, sporting events, historical facts.

* Invite children to help you create bulletin boards. Tell them your theme and ask them to draw maps, collect pictures and other data to display for the class.

* Encourage parent-child projects for some children. These can be effective in cases where parents understand the assignment, when parents have adequate time to assist (working parents may need extended deadlines), where parents are eager to get involved.

* Ask children to help you compile a list of people who have a resource to share with the staff at your school. Place a completed list in the office or the media at your school.

* Have children collect information about places near the school for possible field trip destinations. Share the information and make a class decision about the trip.

* Invite parents to share family vacations (field trips) with the class.

GA1146

SPECTACULAR SPELLING

SPELLING can be one of the most boring classes to the talented student. To the slow learner, it is a class most often dreaded, bringing with it embarrassment and frustration. To the teacher, it is sometimes viewed as a class of lesser importance, to which less time is devoted and taught in a rather plain fashion. To capture the enthusiasm of all people concerned, try a few of the ideas presented here. Vary your lessons to make them more exciting and challenging to all students!

BINGO

Give each child a blank Bingo board and some chips. Ask him to write one spelling word in each square. If you use this activity the first day, simply call out the word for children to cover with a marker. This will familiarize children with their spelling words. Later in the week, state the definition and let children cover the spelling word you defined. Reward winners.

CHEERS

Select the most difficult word on the spelling list. Create a simple cheer with motions that will spell the word. Teach it to your class the first day the word is introduced. This will build confidence to make other list words appear simple. Encourage other children to make up cheers and teach the class, either with or without motions. You may want to let children select teams to create/perform cheers.

GA1146

BINGO

GA1146

SPELLING POSTERS

Divide your class into groups and provide each group with a large piece of mural or poster paper. Ask them to create a poster using words from a specific spelling list. (Review lists are great for this task.) Ideas they may wish to use could include scrambled words, fill-in-the-blanks, word hunts, riddles, matching words/definitions, crossword puzzles. Let groups exchange posters when completed.

WRITE TO SPELL

Good handwriting is essential to good spelling. Select some letter combinations found in list words that are troublesome. Isolate these letters and have children practice writing them on paper, on the chalkboard, using ink, or any other technique you can think of to encourage children to practice writing them. Examples: *ou, ow, ri, ve, ue*

CHALK ONE UP

Often children do not get much experience writing on the chalkboard. Let groups of children go to the board one group at a time to take a pretest, take a posttest, take dictation of sentences, create sentences, make word chains from list words (example: cook-precook-cooks-cooked), illustrate spelling words, create codes/puzzles, make several little words from a spelling word. Stress neatness on the chalkboard as well as on paper.

GA1146

VERTICAL SPELLING

Select a spelling word and write it vertically on the chalkboard. Now choose a category, perhaps one your class has been studying: capitals, nouns, adverbs, Presidents, animals, etc. Ask children to give you a word from the category selected that begins with each letter in the spelling word. Write these answers horizontally beside the letters in the spelling word.

LETTER-BY-LETTER RELAY

Many children are bored during spelling bees because there is a long wait between turns. Let each row of desks or tables be a team. Give one team a word. Have each child spell one letter, with the next child giving the next letter, and so on. This promotes good listening, since letters or words cannot be repeated by you or the person who just spelled. If the word is spelled correctly, give the team as many points as there are letters in the word.

CLASSIFY

Give each child a copy of the CLASSIFICATION work sheet. Have him use his spelling list words to complete the categories suggested. Design your own classification work sheets using concepts stressed on specific spelling lists. Encourage children to create similar activities.

PLURALS

_____

_____

_____

_____

_____

ANTONYMS

SYLLABLES

3

2

1

SYNONYMS

_____

_____

_____

_____

_____

CLASSIFICATION WORK SHEET

_____

NAME

The secret to encouraging children to succeed in spelling is to keep them motivated through a variety of techniques and learning activities. Below are ways you can INDIVIDUALIZE spelling in your classroom to meet the needs of different learning abilities.

INDIVIDUALIZE SPELLING

- Label objects in your classroom you want your children to learn to spell. Remove labels when children have mastered the words and place the labels in a container at a learning center for reinforcement throughout the year.

- Place spelling games in a corner of your room for children to play when work is completed. Examples: Boggle, Wheel of Fortune, Probe, Scrabble

- Establish a buddy system. Select compatible learning partners to help each other with assignments, oral spelling, chalkboard activities (Hangman, pretests, etc.)

- Provide each child with a special notebook or spelling booklet. When a child has completed a writing/creative writing assignment for you, circle words he has misspelled. Ask him to spell them correctly in his notebook to use as a resource for later written assignments. (Have children cut pictures from old magazines and paste one per sheet onto notebook paper. Use the pictures to inspire children to write stories. That way you are encouraging them to write about their interests, and spelling words will be appropriate to their vocabulary as they express their thoughts about topics they have chosen.)

GA1146

- Compile additional spelling lists around seasonal, monthly, student, or content-oriented themes. These words can be learned weekly, monthly, or whatever way you feel is appropriate for your students. These words will challenge and interest most students, since the words are used to supplement the basal text. Bonus points can be given for words mastered, and recorded on a motivational-type chart for others to see.

You may wish to organize these spelling lists in CONTRACT FORM, as seen on page 81. Use the ideas provided or supply your own activities.

Here are ideas for lists you may want to try.
1. Famous people (inventors, entertainers, authors, Presidents, athletes)
2. Famous places (vacation spots, historical places)
3. Colors
4. Names of teams (baseball, basketball, hockey, football)
5. Places around town (malls, restaurants, theaters, stores, parks, museums)
7. Names of days/months/holidays
8. Kinds of transportation
9. Name of toys
10. Fashion designers
11. Sports
12. Geographical terms (river, peninsula, isthmus, country, continent, capital, gulf, bay)
13. Kinds of animals
14. Names of states or countries/capitals
15. Names of TV shows or cartoon characters
16. Names of food
17. Types of plants (flowers, trees)
18. Names of careers
19. Words for a specific content area (planets, oceanography, communication, geometry)

SPELLING CONTRACT

1. school
2. principal
3. classroom
4. office
5. custodian
6. teacher
7. student
8. cafeteria
9. library
10. desk
11. hall
12. backpack
13. schedule
14. class
15. recess
16. pencil
17. paper
18. ruler
19. scissors
20. book
21. glue
22. social studies
23. physical education
24. math
25. science
26. art
27. music
28. spelling
29. reading
30. language

Mon.

1. Write words 1-30 in list form on your paper. Beside each word write the plural.
2. Write a sentence using any fifteen of your list words.

Tues.

Use an old magazine or newspaper. Cut out entire words or letters to spell your spelling words. Glue them to paper.

Wed.

Use graph paper. Create a word hunt by writing the words forward, backward, diagonally in your best printing. Write your words below the word search for children to use as answers.

Thurs.

Choose at least twenty spelling words to write in alphabetical order. Skip three lines between each word. Now draw pictures of each word for your picture dictionary. Color them.

Fri.

Organize and label all of your work for the week. Take your spelling test. Give your teacher your test and all of the work except the word hunt. Exchange the word hunt with a friend to solve.

GA1146

Motivate your children with these creative math ideas. Use them to supplement your daily curriculum. Use them to reinforce skills taught, or use them to individualize your daily instruction.

MARVELOUS MATH

After your children understand the math concept you are teaching, give each child a manila folder in which he will keep all of his assignments. On the cover, have him write his name and add a design. Inside the cover on the left-hand side, have him record five to ten assignments you wish him to do to reinforce that skill.

Example: 1 _____ page 25 (problems 1-10). In the space after the number, you record the grade for that assignment. Children can work at their own pace and you can readily see progress.

Give each child a copy of the Bingo card found on page 75. Have him write any numbers from 0-100 in the spaces. You may want to use numbers 0-25 or 0-50, depending on the age of the student and the skill you are stressing. Play the game to reinforce math facts (addition, subtraction, multiplication, division).

Make several copies of the gameboard The Math Magician. Have children bring small gameboard markers from home or use small objects they have. You determine the concept by having children make small flash cards for a particular skill. Place simple concepts in even stack on gameboard and more difficult problems in the odd pile. Provide time for children to play the game. They will need a die or spinner to determine number of spaces moved.

Have a math bee in the same fashion you would a spelling bee. Mental math is not often stressed, so this is a great way to involve your students. Ask math facts, story problems, or math methods pertaining to skills on which you are working. When a child answers incorrectly, have him solve the problem on the board. If it is a math fact, you may want him to write it several times on the board.

SHAPELY FASHIONS is a fun exercise to do. Use it to reinforce geometric shapes (circle, square, triangle, rectangle). Divide the class into groups, placing four to five children in each group. Ask them to see how many shapes their group can find on clothing and write them down to later share with the class (examples: rectangular belt buckle, round treads on shoes, round shoe eyelets, square eyeglasses). Reward the group with the most answers.

GA1146

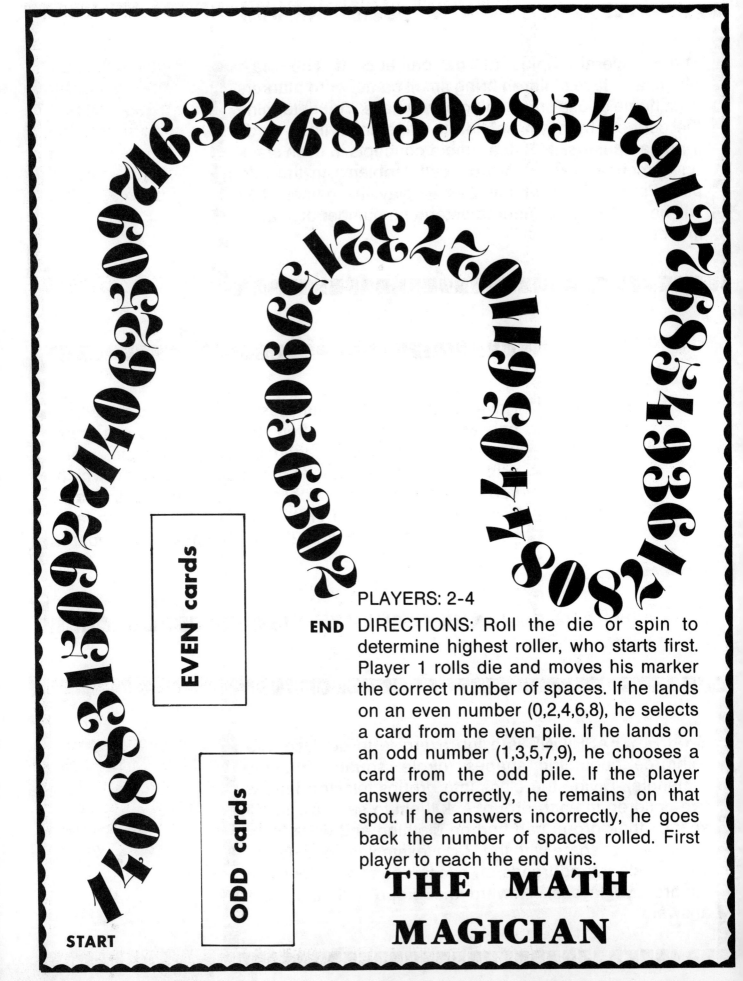

PLAYERS: 2-4

END DIRECTIONS: Roll the die or spin to determine highest roller, who starts first. Player 1 rolls die and moves his marker the correct number of spaces. If he lands on an even number (0,2,4,6,8), he selects a card from the even pile. If he lands on an odd number (1,3,5,7,9), he chooses a card from the odd pile. If the player answers correctly, he remains on that spot. If he answers incorrectly, he goes back the number of spaces rolled. First player to reach the end wins.

THE MATH MAGICIAN

EVEN cards

ODD cards

START

Try a game of Musical Math. It is played similar to Musical Chairs, but you may want to remove more than one chair at the start of the game. When the music stops, children without chairs go to the chalkboard to solve a problem you give them. If they answer correctly, they stay in the game and receive NO points. If a child answers incorrectly, he stays in the game, but earns a point. Children with NO points are winners!

RAT RACE is a game to encourage *speed with accuracy*! Use the chalkboard, computer, calculator, or paper/ pencil to see which students answer correctly first. This can be played with teams or partners. It's a great way to challenge talented children and reinforce basic skills. Keep track of winners by charts, classroom motivators (see pages 55-63).

The PITTER PATTERN activity sheet is designed for individual or team use. Give a copy to the child and ask him to find numbers that form equations either vertically, horizontally, or diagonally. Have him circle the answers with colored marker or pen. Older children may be able to find examples of numerous math concepts, while younger children may use only one skill.

GA1146

PITTER PATTERN

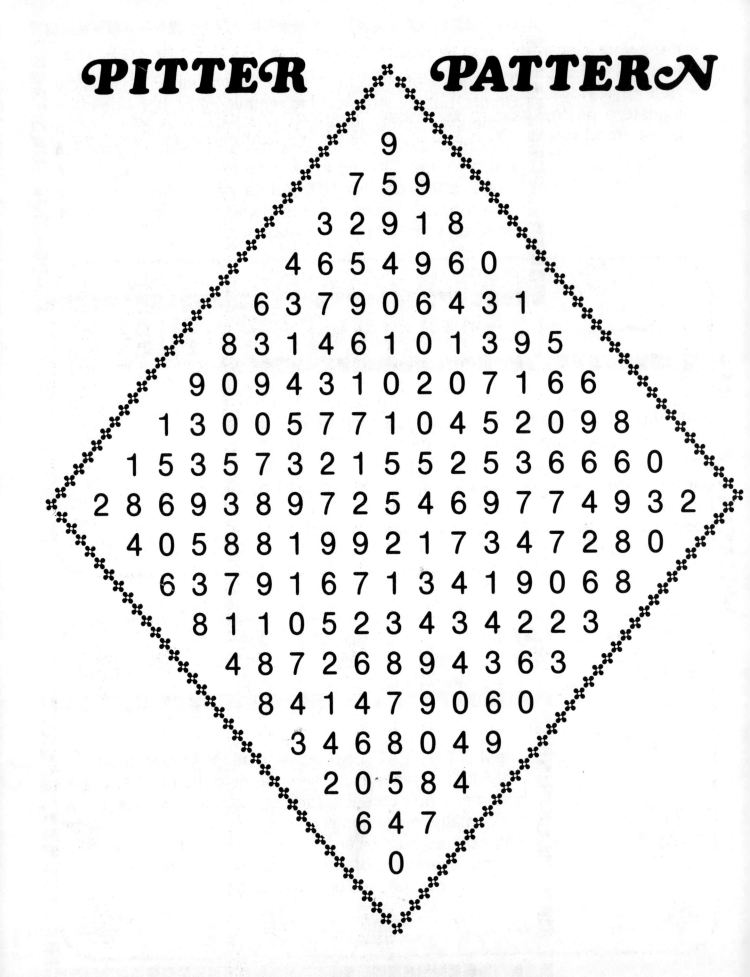

Keep your classroom organized with these handy TEACHER PASSES. The first one has been labeled for you. Label the second one to suit your needs: Hall Pass, Boys'/Girls' Bathroom Pass, Library Pass. Be sure to write your signature on the pass to verify that it belongs to you. If it is lost, it can be returned to you. Color and label the passes before you laminate them.

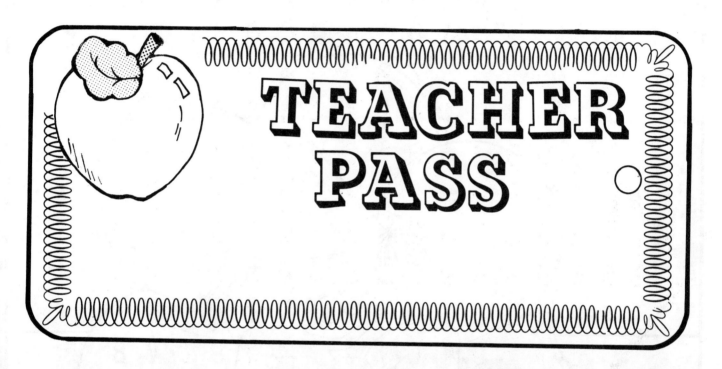

GA1146

Birthday Card

Color and cut out the pop-up birthday card. Cut along the balloons on the dotted lines. Press card closed along the fold lines. Add your birthday greeting inside. Your card is now ready to send to that special person.

HAPPY BIRTHDAY !

GA1146

Cut out the Fold-a-Card along the heavy solid line. On the outside of the card, write your return address in the upper left-hand corner. In the center, address the card to the person you wish to thank. Add a stamp. Record your message inside or use page 90. Glue the seal and mail.

from:_____
_____
_____

Stamp

★   to:_____

_____

_____

Glue

89

Xerox this page on the reverse side of the Thank You Fold-a-Card (page 89) if you choose. If not, write your own message on the inside of the thank-you card.

THANK YOU

Dear _____

Thank you for your kindness,
And the thoughtful things you do;
Thank you for your friendship,
And thanks for being YOU.

From _____

GA1146

PLAY TIME

SEPTEMBER

					1	2
6	7	8	9			
14	15	16				
						23
	28	29	30			

Your children will love the two themes that are interwoven in this section. The Calendar unit will acquaint students with the many concepts associated with it through the numerous activities presented; the Scarecrow unit presents "fall"ow up approach to a plentiful feast of ideas. Supplement the units with finger plays, stories, songs, and other resources of your own.

91

Mother's Tale

"I'm tired," said Little Scarecrow. "I've been standing all day while the sun warmed the fields. Please, may I rest now?"

"Put your arms down," whispered Mother. "Let's sit for a moment. Just lean your head on my shoulder."

When the moon rose, Little Scarecrow begged, "Tell me a story, Mother."

Mother thought for a minute and then softly began. "A very, very long time ago your great great grandparents were born. A farmer fashioned them from two crossed sticks and old clothing. Then he stuffed their bodies with straw. They stood day and night watching the cornfield, trying to protect it from birds and other animals which might destroy the crops. If the crops were ruined, the farmer and his family might starve to death during the winter. Sometimes large flocks would swoop near the fields, and Great Great Grandpa would have to make a lot of noise to get the birds to fly away. Great Great Grandma would flap her arms wildly until the birds disappeared. Even their children learned to do the job well, and they stood for hours guarding the cornfields, too! It was difficult work, but they were pleased because the farmer seemed happy and his fields were healthy.

"But one day, Uncle Oliver, their son, had the scare of his life. It was a hot day in July and he was nearly wilted from the heat. The field had been quiet, so Uncle Oliver decided to sit down. Before long, he fell asleep. As he lay dozing, he dreamed thousands of birds were coming toward him. There were so many that the sky turned dark. And no matter how much noise he made, they ignored him. He was only a scarecrow! Uncle Oliver shouted, but they didn't seem to hear him. Suddenly he felt the earth shake. It vibrated more and more until Uncle Oliver was awakened. And there, racing toward his resting body, hidden in the tall corn, steamed the farmer's tractor. Of course the farmer didn't see Uncle Oliver because he was lying down, hidden in the tall rows of corn. Luckily, just before the farmer whizzed by, Uncle Oliver stood brave and tall, and the tractor swerved from his path."

"That taught Uncle Oliver a lesson, didn't it, Mother?"

"Yes, Little Scarecrow. And we must remember Uncle Oliver's story, too!"

"Tell me another story, please," insisted Little Scarecrow. "And this time make it longer!"

Once again Mother started her tale.

"Early one spring morning, cousin Russell, feeling curious, decided to play along the riverbank. He carefully slipped his arms off the straight stick. How good it felt to just let them dangle at his side! Next, he carefully lifted

GA1146

his body from the tall stick that supported his back. Slowly he bent over to touch his toes. His little body was stiff from staying in the same position for a long, long time. His little head flopped down, and the felt hat he'd been wearing dropped to the ground. Russell realized it just might take him a while to get to the river. He stretched his body toward the water where it whirled between smooth, round stones. He inched a little closer and a little closer, hoping to touch the cool, clear water. His eyes had watched the water for several days, and this morning he just HAD to get in it. At the water's edge, Russell paused, fascinated. First, he put in his leg. The water tickled! Before long both legs were wet. Russell was so excited about this adventure that he had forgotten about his clothes. The water was waist high, and his clothes stuck to his body of straw. They felt so funny! Russell tried to balance, but the water was pulling him along. He was moving away from shore, and now his arms were soaked. He tried to swim toward the riverbank, but his clothes sagged under the weight of the water. "If I could just get to the edge, he thought." With difficulty, he tried to pick up one leg and step forward. Just when he got it raised a little, the water pushed him over and he was carried downstream. The cornfield along the shore was nothing but a blur. Faster and faster went Russell. His body felt lighter as the current moved him along. When Russell looked down, his arms were getting smaller and smaller. Hay was floating all around him. Then he realized that he was coming apart. His thin legs were twirling around on the surface. Just then Russell felt a bump. He had been pushed into an old tree which lay fallen along the riverbank. His body had drifted into the branches and had gotten stuck. Lying on his back and tangled along the trunk, Russell looked toward the blue sky overhead. He sure hadn't meant for this to happen! He just wanted to explore by the river! After a while, the sun began to warm his little straw face. Even the straw covering the rest of his body stiffened as the heat penetrated his wet clothing. "If I could just get myself out of this mess and stand up," Russell thought. "Then I could walk back home. And I would never leave my post again!"

"Before long the sun began to set, and the spring air sent cold chills through Russell's body. How he wished he was on dry land, guarding his cornfield like a responsible scarecrow! Just then he heard voices—children's voices. Closer and closer they came. On the other side of the tree they stopped and began to hook something on the end of a string. Then they took a long stick and jerked one end toward the water. The string came loose, so they reeled it in with a little crank. "I wonder what they're doing? They keep throwing and reeling. If they would talk a little louder, perhaps I might understand," thought Russell. "Ouch! That boy hit me with something!"

93

GA1146

"Rushing over to the old tree, the boy followed his string. He tugged. As he stepped a little closer to pull it loose, his eyes focused on the tangled mass of straw. And then he saw the clothes! What was this thing he was looking at? Cautiously, he bent over to examine it a little more carefully. The eyes were watching him! The little boy yelled to his friend. Together they lifted the frail body from the river and placed it on the grassy bank. They'd never had a scarecrow watch them fish before! After a long while, the boys disappeared, leaving Russell to dry on the grassy bank.

"I've got to get home," Russell worried. His straw was firm now. His clothes were dry. He began scurrying along, following the river, and hoping it would lead him home. It seemed like he had walked for hours. Tired, Russell sat down to rest, wondering where his home was. As he stood up, he looked back into the cornfield. Each row looked the same. Just then Russell discovered his hat! "My hat! My hat!" he exclaimed. He put in on. Now he wouldn't have to squint in the bright sunlight. Now his head would be warm at night! Russell walked a few steps into the cornfield and found the cross that marked his home. Cheerfully, he climbed to the top of the stick and slid his arms into position. "Home at last," sighed Russell. Russell was so weak from his adventure, and he had lost so much weight. But he was happy to be safe back in the cornfield. As his eyes studied the rows and rows of corn, Russell could see where the birds had been eating. Right now they were playing overhead. "It will take me awhile to get my strength back, but when I do, I'll hold my head high, I'll stand tall and proud, and I'll never, NEVER leave again!"

"Little Scarecrow? Little Scarecrow?" whispered Mother.

But Little Scarecrow was fast asleep.

GA1146

Let's Think About...

1. What is the purpose of a scarecrow?_____

_____

_____

2. What materials can be used to make scarecrows?

_____

_____

_____

3. Describe some of the "scarecrows" you have seen.

_____

_____

_____

4. Can you think of ways that farmers protect their crops other than by using scarecrows? _____

_____

_____

_____

Draw pictures and color them.

5.

UNCLE OLIVER

6.

RUSSELL

The Scarecrow's Secret

Characters:
Narrator
Scarecrow
Pumpkin 1
Pumpkin 2
Pumpkin 3
Pumpkins (singers and dancers)
Crow 1
Crow 2
Crow 3
Crows (other students in class)

Scene I

(In the farmer's cornfield)

Scarecrow:	(Sings slowly to tune of "Twinkle, Twinkle, Little Star")

I have got an old straw hat
Sitting on my floppy head.
I am wearing worn-out clothes
From the Farmer's Uncle Ted.
Look at my old flannel shirt.
See my patched-up faded jeans.
I sure try to keep the birds
Out of the pumpkins, corn, and beans.

Crow 1:	Look at this field! It's perfect!
All Crows:	(Circle field and scatter around Scarecrow)
Crow 2:	Seeds! (Some Crows move around)
Crow 3:	Lots of seeds! (More crows move around to get seeds)
Scarecrow:	Shoo! Shoo, I say! (Waves arms)

96

All Crows:	(Fly away)
Scarecrow:	(Makes crying sound)
Crow 1:	(Flies onto stage) What's that I hear? (Cocks his head and listens)
Crows 2, 3:	(Fly in by Crow 1)

Crow 2:	A cry? (Hops over near Scarecrow)
Crow 3:	You're only a scarecrow! Why are you crying?
Scarecrow:	I'm lonesome! (Continues to cry) I keep the farmer happy, but I'm not happy. I have no friends!
Pumpkin 1:	I'll be your friend. I need water to make me grow. Will you share your tears with me?
Pumpkin 2:	My vines will grow so strong. They will hold your body straight.
Scarecrow:	(Cries again)
Pumpkin 3:	Water will help me grow big and round. Then I can keep you warm at night.
Scarecrow:	I'm happy I can help you. I've saved these tears for a long, long time.
Some Crows:	(Fly near scarecrow and land)
Scarecrow:	(Cries again, then sees crows) Shoo!

GA1146

Crow 1:	(Hops closer and looks at Scarecrow) Your body is made of straw!
Scarecrow:	Shoo! (Sobbing)
Crows 2, 3:	We need straw for our nest!
Scarecrow:	Straw? MY straw? I can help you?
Crows 1, 2, 3:	Of course you can! (Take straw from Scarecrow and begin to build a nest toward the center/side of stage)
All Crows:	(Begin to build a nest and settle in)
Scarecrow:	(Cries again)
Crow 2:	What's the matter? Did we hurt you?
Scarecrow:	No! No! I'm just so happy.
Crows:	You're happy?
Pumpkins:	Are WE still your friends?
Scarecrow:	I hope we will always be friends.

98

GA1146

All Pumpkins: (Sing song to the tune of "Yellow Rose of Texas" as they
(except 1, 2, 3)   sit in a row along front edge of stage. They will be seated
                       here during entire performance.)

Song/Dance (Children move from sitting position into circle)

(Line 1)   We are tiny little pumpkins who would like to grow so round,
                (Children walk clockwise in circle)

(Line 2)   Please give us light and water, and we'll be the best in town.
                (Children walk counterclockwise in circle)

(Line 3)   Our stems will be so sturdy and our bodies orange and bright,
                (Children hook right elbows and swing partner)

(Line 4)   Now just you watch this pumpkin patch. See what a gorgeous
                sight! (Children hook left elbows and swing partner)

(At the end of the music, children sit comfortably around Scarecrow and
Crows caw softly from their nest.)

GA1146

Props:

1. A mask for each character in the play (see pattern pages 101-105)
2. Appropriate Scarecrow clothing to suit description in the song
3. Straw for Scarecrow and Crow's nest
4. Tape recorder (optional) to accompany children as Pumpkins sing
5. Hay bales (optional) to add decor to stage
6. Seeds or beans (lima beans would work)

Notes:

1. Be sure to seat all Pumpkins (except 1, 2, 3) across front of stage during entire performance.
2. Make Pumpkins dance simpler or more difficult to suit needs of your class.
3. Verse 1 for the dance could include words and music, while verse 2 could be only the accompaniment while children repeat dance.
4. Place Scarecrow halfway back to the left of stage front.

Comments:

GA1146

Scarecrow

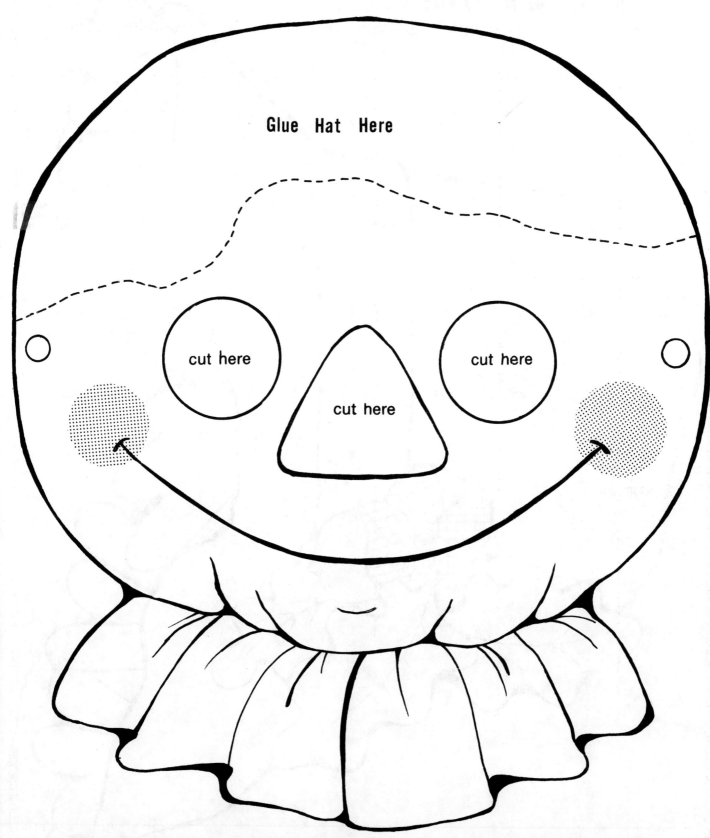

Glue Hat Here

cut here

cut here

cut here

Make mask from white or manila oaktag. Color as desired. Attach oaktag hat using pattern on the following page. (You may wish to use only the face pattern and have child wear a real straw hat.) Add a string tie when mask is completely dry.

GA1146

Scarecrow's Hat

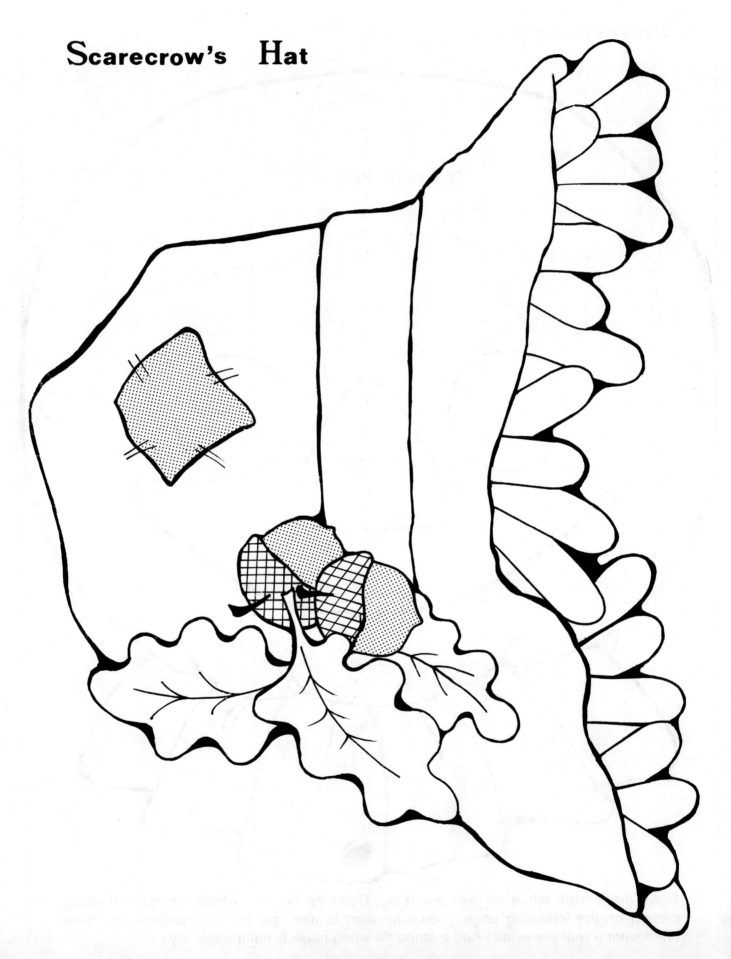

102

GA1146

Pumpkin

cut here

cut here

cut here

103

Crow

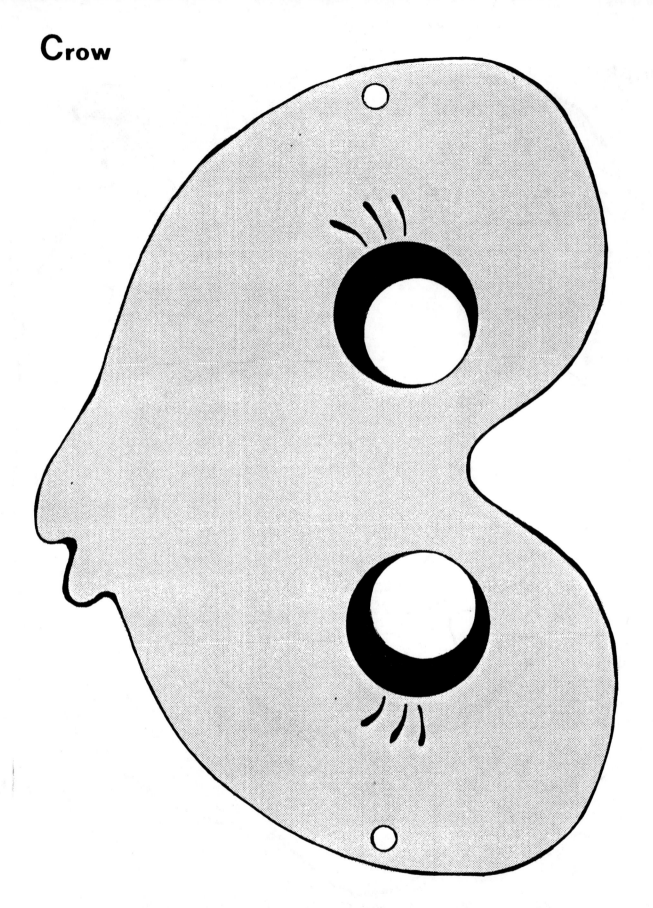

Make mask from black oaktag or construction paper. Cut the beak (page 105) from heavy orange paper. Fold the beak on the dotted line. Put glue on the top shaded area of beak and attach crow's beak to the black face mask. Let dry completely before handling. Attach yarn or string to hold the mask in place.

GA1146

Crow's Beak

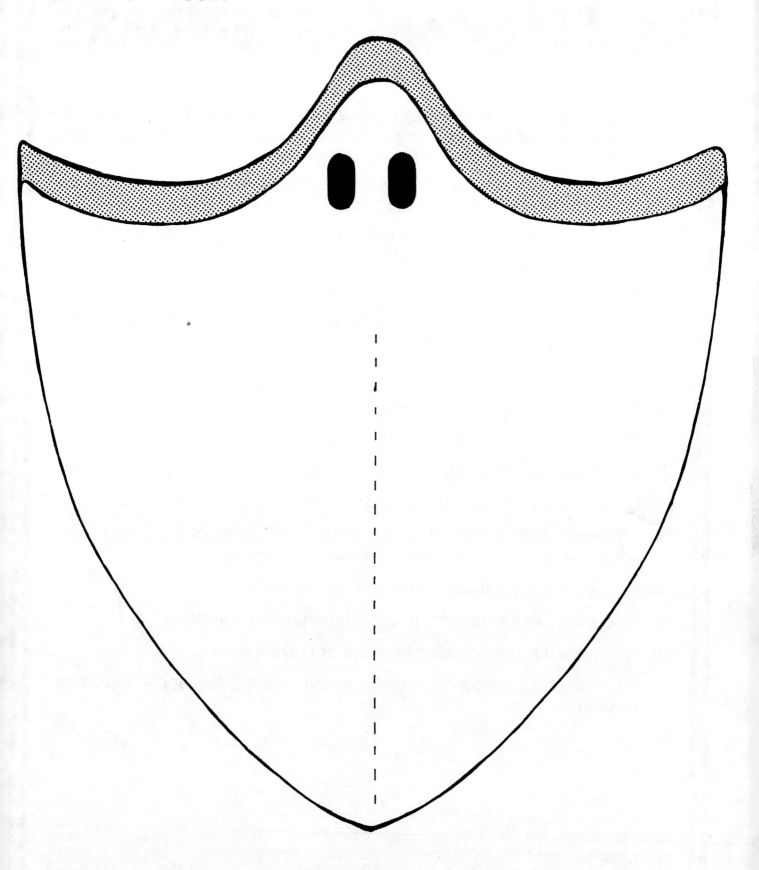

105

GA1146

CLASSROOM CALENDARS

Calendars decorate the walls and desks in many classrooms. They come in various sizes, shapes, and price ranges. For these reasons, calendars make terrific teaching tools at all learning levels.

On pages 107-108 you will find actual activity calendars. These can be created easily by you and adapted to any skill in any content area.

Here are numerous ways that you can use the calendar in your classroom. (This can be done on a group calendar displayed in the front of the room or on individual calendars for each student.)

1. To teach names, spellings, and abbreviations of the days of the week, months of the year

2. To teach number sequence

3. To discuss concepts of weekday/weekend

4. To discuss concepts of yesterday/today/tomorrow

5. To identify special holidays, class birthdays

6. To schedule children into learning centers

7. To record daily events, current events, coming attractions (diary form, assignments, school programs, family happenings)

8. To predict/record the weather

9. To display "Helper for the Day," "Job Helpers for the Week"

10. To initiate discussion about holidays or current events

11. To encourage student research about monthly/seasonal topics of interest

GA1146

ALL AROUND TOWN

SUN.	MON.	TUES.	WED.	THURS.	FRI.	SAT.
	Name as many buildings in your town as you can.	Make up several rules you feel people in your town should follow.	List all the places children your age like to go to in your town.	Name someone in your town that you admire. Draw a picture of him/her.	Write a paragraph telling why you admire that person. (See yesterday's assignment.)	
	Name as many towns as you can think of near your town. Name any attractions there.	Name several restaurants found in/near your town. Put a * by your favorite one.	Write your favorite restaurant across the top of your paper. List favorite foods you like to order.	When you go to the library in town, what section of books interests you the most? Why?	What would you say is the largest business in town? Tell about it.	
	Think of the ways people in your town travel. Write them down.	Draw and color a picture showing a special event your town has.	Would your town be a good place for a new business? Why or why not?	Write a paragraph telling what new business you would welcome into town.	Design a park for your town. Give it a name.	
	Where could you shop for a new school outfit? Draw the clothes you would buy.	Write down a famous landmark or familiar place in town. Tell something about it.	Does your town have a hospital? Name the one closest to you.	Write down the name of your school. List five good comments about it.	Invent a festival for your town. Give it a name. Choose the date. Explain the events.	
	Name all the businesses you can think of in your town.	Categorize the businesses you thought of yesterday—restaurants, banks, etc.	Pretend that you named your town. In a paragraph, tell why you chose the name.	Name at least ten streets in your town.	Where can you go to take special classes other than your school?	

107

GA1146

MY CLASS

SUN.	MON.	TUES.	WED.	THURS.	FRI.	SAT.
	Draw a picture of the greatest place you've ever been. Label it.	Write a note to your teacher telling him/her something about yourself.	What is your favorite color? Write it at the top of your paper. List ten or more things that are the same color.	If you could be an animal, what animal would you be and why?	Write a letter to your teacher stating topics you would like to study this year.	
	Write the names of any ten children in your class using your best handwriting.	Write the ten names you wrote yesterday in ABC order.	How many boys are in the class? How many girls? How many students in all?	Find out who in your class has a birthday this month. Record their names and their birthdates.	Think about your favorite hobby. List several reasons why you enjoy it.	
	Interview a classmate to find out what his favorite hobby is. Write a paragraph about the results of the interview.	Make a list of all types of shoes your classmates are wearing. After each, tell how children are wearing that style.	Think about your favorite book. Write the title of the book on a piece of paper. Then illustrate a scene.	Color the scene you drew yesterday. Be neat.	List all of the classes you're taking this year. Begin with your favorite class and continue to your least favorite.	
	Print your teacher's name across the top of your paper. See how many words you can make from those letters.	Try writing your full name at least fifteen different ways on your paper.	Make a list of several qualities that you feel make a good teacher.	Make your paper look like this: alike | different Show how you and your friend are alike/different.	Write a paragraph about your favorite school subject. State reasons why you like it.	
	Draw a picture of one of your happiest memories. Color it.	Write sentences, a paragraph or a short story explaining your happiest memory.	Think about yourself. Name at least five qualities you have that make people want to be your friend.	Find out who are the oldest and youngest members of your class.	Draw a picture showing where you would like to take a field trip with your class.	

GA1146

CREATE A CALENDAR

- Reinforce skills previously taught
- Encourage independent activity
- Stimulate interest in a variety of content areas

Try a little classroom fun! Make copies of the calendar for each child. (Add your own activities on the blank calendar pages.) Compile the pages into a book and attach with yarn ties. This calendar is based on a scarecrow theme. You may want to plan activities for the weekends, also. In that case, you will need ideas for 28-31 days of fun. Ask children to record correct dates for the month in the appropriate spaces on the pages. Schedule a specific time each day, perhaps first thing in the morning, when you want children to complete the particular assignment.

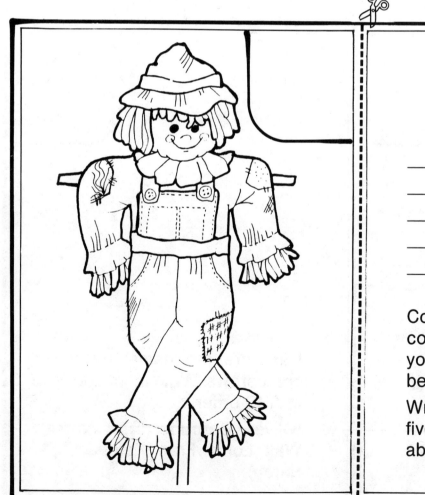

Color the scarecrow on the cover of your calendar. Write your name on the cover in your best handwriting.

Write your scarecrow's name five times neatly on the lines above.

GA1146

In the space below, list several feelings your scarecrow might have. After each answer, write why you think it has these feelings.

Think about the scarecrow on the cover of your booklet. Write five good sentences about him/her.

S
C
A
R
E
C
R
O
W
_____
_____
_____
_____
_____
_____
_____
_____
_____

An *adjective* is a word that describes something. Write an adjective about your scarecrow for each letter above. Your *acrostic* poem is now complete.

Here are the names of ten scarecrows. Write them above in ABC order.

(Oliver, Gertrude, Tim, Zack, Walt, Louis, Fran, Kate, Josh, Sarah)

A *verb* is an action word. It tells something you can do. List eight verbs below that tell something your scarecrow can do.

_____
_____
_____
_____

If your scarecrow could live anywhere in the world, where would it live and why? Write your answer on the lines above.

Use these words in a paragraph. Be sure to add capital letters and punctuation when necessary.

(farmer, crows, scarecrow, cornfield, idea, happy, autumn)

Pretend that a scarecrow is your best friend. Draw a picture of the two of you doing your favorite hobby.

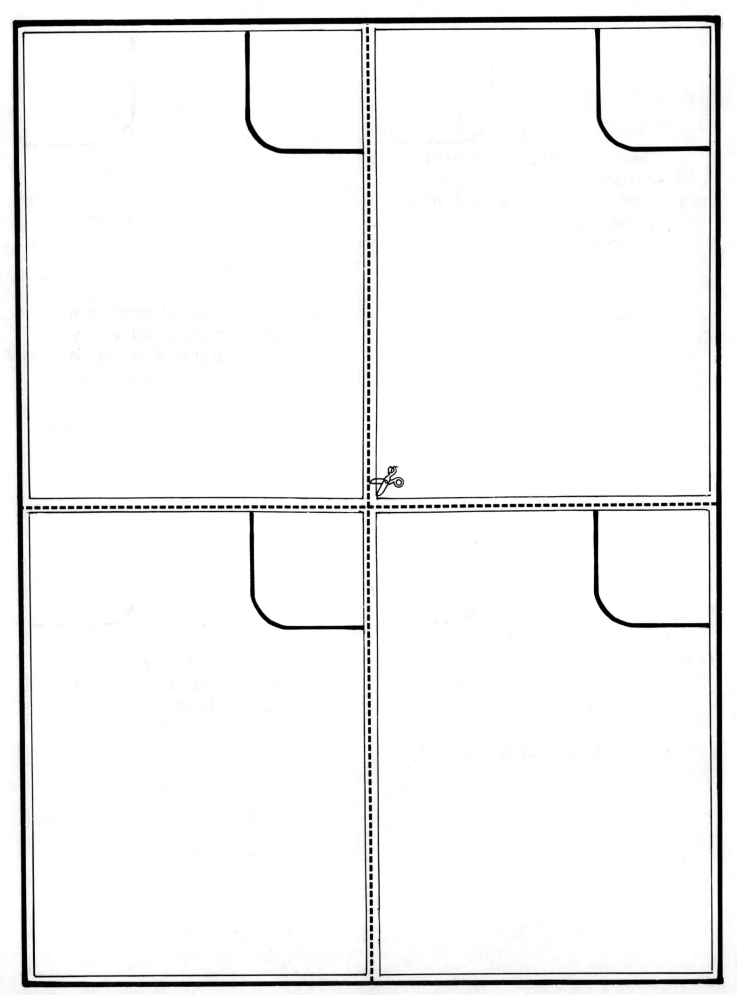

112

SCARECROW MOBILE

What a great way to create atmosphere in your classroom! Use heavy white paper or oaktag and make a copy of the scarecrow mobile patterns for each child.

After each child colors and cuts out his scarecrow, punch holes in the appropriate places so that he can attach yarn or string. Remind him to write his name on the back.

Decorate your ceiling and let the fun begin!

GA1146

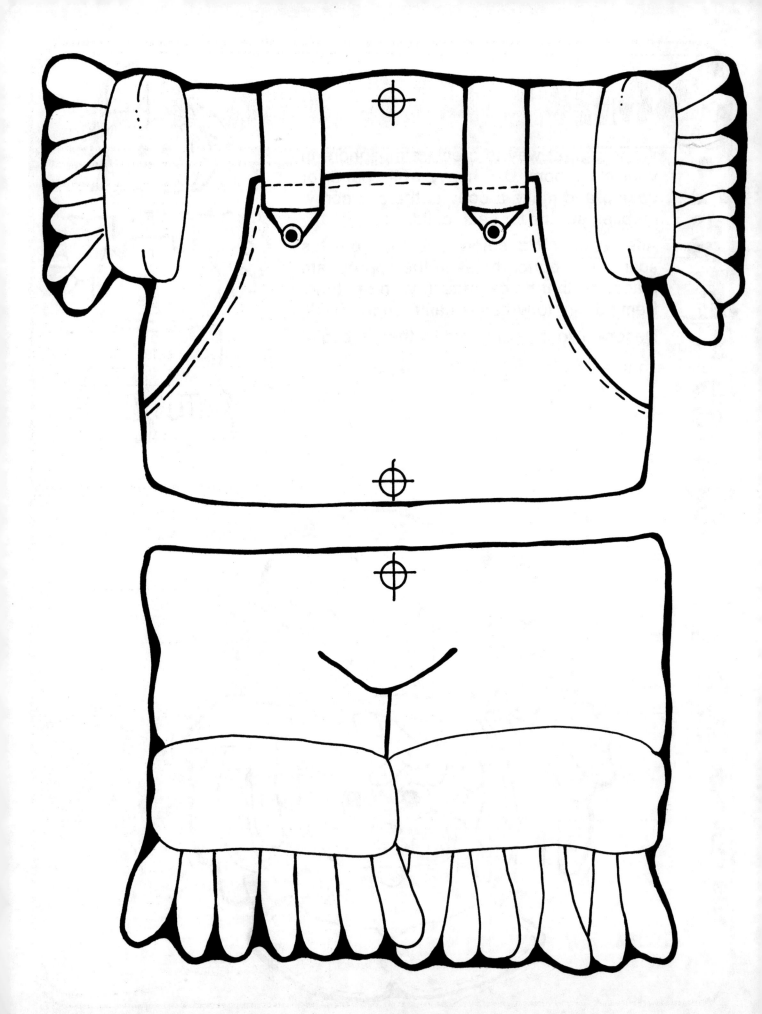

114

SOMETHING FOR FUN

Create a *tongue twister* with as many words as you can beginning with *sc*.

_____

_____

How many words can you make that begin with the letters *sc*?

1. _____
2. _____
3. _____
4. _____
5. _____
6. _____
7. _____
8. _____
9. _____
10. _____
11. _____
12. _____
13. _____
14. _____
15. _____
16. _____
17. _____
18. _____
19. _____
20. _____

Make your second line rhyme with the first line to complete these couplets.

The little scarecrow said

_____

I'll hold my head up tall

_____

I'll scare the birds away

_____

Pretend that the scarecrow sitting below is you. On the lines write about the responsibilities you have.

_____

_____

_____

_____

_____

_____

_____

_____

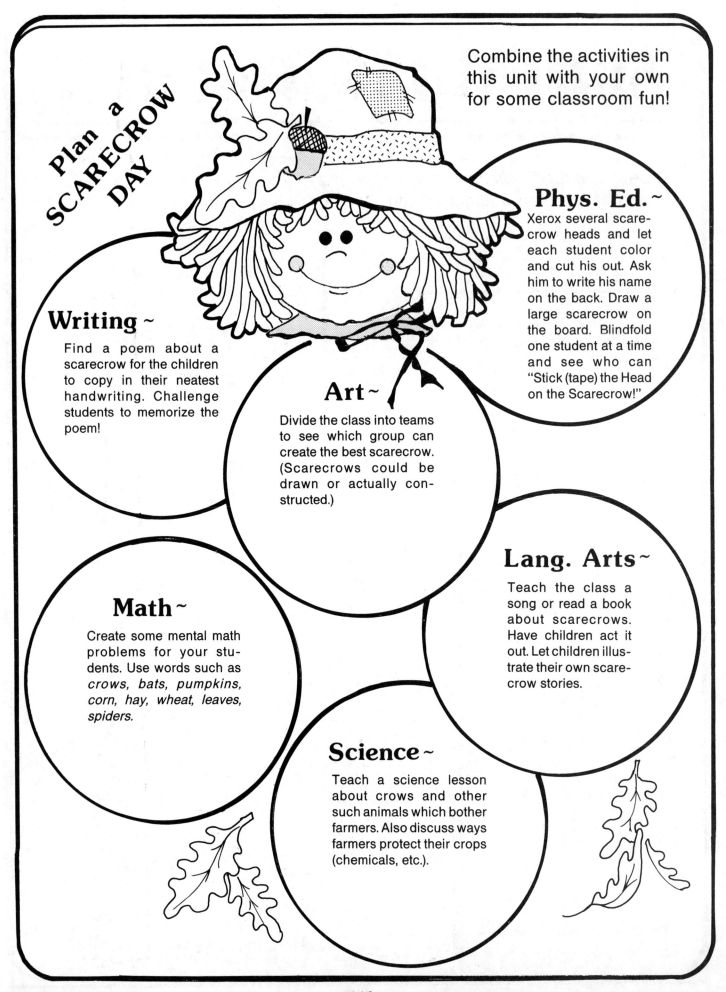

Plan a SCARECROW DAY

Combine the activities in this unit with your own for some classroom fun!

Phys. Ed. ~
Xerox several scarecrow heads and let each student color and cut his out. Ask him to write his name on the back. Draw a large scarecrow on the board. Blindfold one student at a time and see who can "Stick (tape) the Head on the Scarecrow!"

Writing ~
Find a poem about a scarecrow for the children to copy in their neatest handwriting. Challenge students to memorize the poem!

Art ~
Divide the class into teams to see which group can create the best scarecrow. (Scarecrows could be drawn or actually constructed.)

Lang. Arts ~
Teach the class a song or read a book about scarecrows. Have children act it out. Let children illustrate their own scarecrow stories.

Math ~
Create some mental math problems for your students. Use words such as *crows, bats, pumpkins, corn, hay, wheat, leaves, spiders.*

Science ~
Teach a science lesson about crows and other such animals which bother farmers. Also discuss ways farmers protect their crops (chemicals, etc.).

GA1146

PUPPET TREE

Creative Drama Unit

SCHOOL SPIRIT

PUPPET TREE

Combine puppetry and a little dramatics to make this choral reading come to life. Select a narrator to introduce the reading, divide your students into four groups (owls, cats, mice, and spiders) for speaking parts, build the tree stage, then rehearse. Before long your presentation will be polished and ready for an audience!

Owls:
From my perch high in the tree,
I watch the forest carefully,
I sleep by day and hunt by night,
When most people run from fright.
I have a strong beak, watchful eyes,
And fluffy feathers for my disguise.
WHOOOOOO am I? WHOOOOOO, I say,
Is sneaking up my trunk today?

Cats:
I slink along with curious looks
To see what hides in little nooks;
I claw my feet into the bark,
So on that high branch I can park.
My beady eyes are watchful, too,
The higher I go, the better the veiw!

Owls:
WHOOOOOOO is up here in my tree?

Cats:
MEOOOOOW! I growl when I have a scare
That curls my back and raises my hair!

Owls:
What do you want from a wise old owl?
Is that the way you talk, MEOOOOOOOW?

118

GA1146

Cats: I simply meant to purr "meow"
          But when I'm scared it makes a growl.
          And now I'll tell you why I'm here—
          I have an awful, awful fear.
          You see, I must admit my fright—
          I am afraid of—of the night.
          I hear noises 'round the house
          That sound just like a baby—

Mice: EEEEEK! EEEEEK! Did you see that?
          I think it was a pussy cat!
          If he saw me, I'd bet he'd run
          And have himself a little fun.
          He'd lick his lips and twist his nose,
          And then sit gracefully and pose;
          Then in a flash he'd pounce on me,
          And hide me by this old oak tree
          Where I would tease him until night
          And he would lose me. What a sight!
          EEEEEK! I'd scream, "Do you see that?
          I think there goes my pussy cat!"

Cats: MEOOOOOOW! I growl when I have a scare
          That curls my back and raises my hair.

Mice: Back up the tree I follow the growl
          To find that cat by a fluffy owl.
          Dear Mr. Owl, I must confess,
          I shouldn't be here in this mess.
          For a hungry cat would no doubt want dinner,
          And it seems to me, I might be the winner!
          EEEEEK! I scream, "Could you please hide her?
          I'd like to catch myself a . . . ."

GA1146

Owls:	WHOOO! said the owl, WHOOO'd you want me to hide? As he sat looking on, with his mouth opened wide!
Mice:	EEEEEK! EEEEEK! I squeaked loudly As I scurried down the tree. I see a web; it's beautifully spun. Complete with a spider, my work's just begun! A feast I shall have in my neat, cozy hole, I dreamed, as toward the web I stole. My little paws reached out to grab That crafty spider, calm and drab; But there behind my long, gray tail Something echoed throughout the vale.
Owls:	WHOOOO eats who? I began to screech. Look who's now within my reach! That little spider's spent all day Spinning threads to catch her prey. She sits and waits so patiently— A lesson for us all to see!
Spiders:	My tired legs need lots of rest. This busy body did its best To decorate your old oak tree, So daintily for all to see. If you would eat me, you would miss Your pretty home, with all its bliss— So, Mr. Owl, I ask of you, To let me make my home here, too!
Owl:	This tree holds secrets, that I know, You forest animals tell me so— If I'm as wise as people say, My home shall be your place to stay. I'll welcome you with open wings, Please come to tell me everything.
Tree:	So all you creatures, great and small, Come! Winter, spring, summer, and fall.

GA1146

Props:

1. A puppet for each student in the play. (See pages 123-125, 128-129, 132-133, 136-137 for cat, mouse, owl, and spider patterns.)
2. A colorful tree to be the puppet stage
3. Tape recorder (optional) to accompany any sounds you might wish to add
4. Spiderweb to attach to the tree

Notes:

1. Use heavy cardboard and make a tall, sturdy tree to be the stage.
2. Choose one student to be leader for each group. Place these children near or behind the tree to perform with the tree stage.
3. Seat the other children on the stage with their puppets. They can stand around the tree when it is their turn to perform.
4. If children cannot memorize the script, attach their lines to the backs of their puppets.
5. Select one student to be the narrator.
6. Rehearse the play with a lot of expression so that the children are confident with animal sounds.
7. Ask one student to be the voice of the tree. (This could be the same person as the narrator.)

Comments:

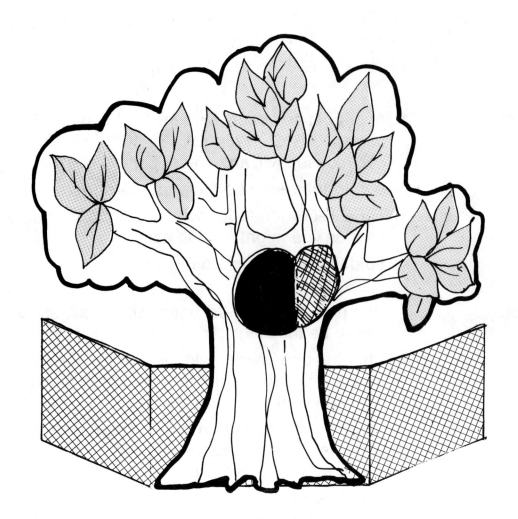

SETTING THE STAGE

Your choral reading, designed for puppets, would not be complete without a stage—a tree stage. This simple stage can be designed of cardboard or plywood. The window(s) are partially cut and swing forward, allowing a few students to act out their parts. The sides of the set-like stage on either side of the tree provide further acting space for the puppets. Students will enjoy painting and designing this simple stage!

GA1146

TUBE PUPPETS

spider's
face

Four paper tube puppet patterns have been included to use with the choral reading found on pages 118-120. Patterns included are Spider, Cat, Mouse, and Owl. These puppets are easy to create and will thrill the children as they prepare to dramatize the choral reading. The tube puppets are designed around a simple tube shape, formed by rolling the pattern into a tube and attaching a face and other body parts provided. Simply insert your hand in the tube and the puppets will come to life!

You might want to have children dramatize individual scenes, skits, or impromptu ideas they created. Have students perform them for you to become familiar with their puppets, and to practice acting in front of the class.

GA1146

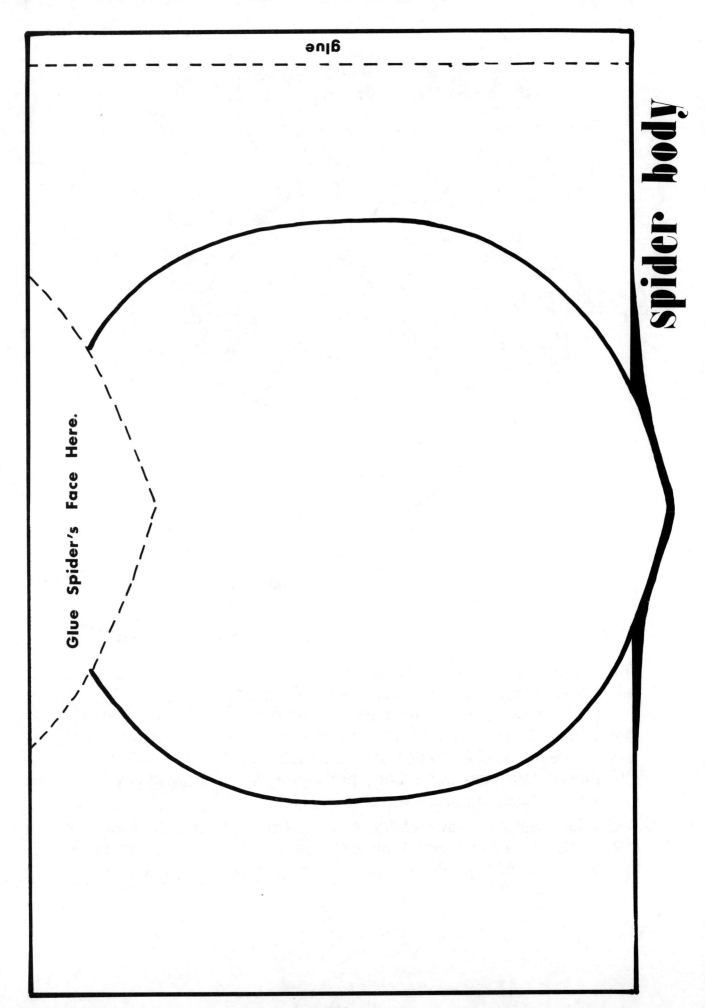

spider body

glue

Glue Spider's Face Here.

GA1146

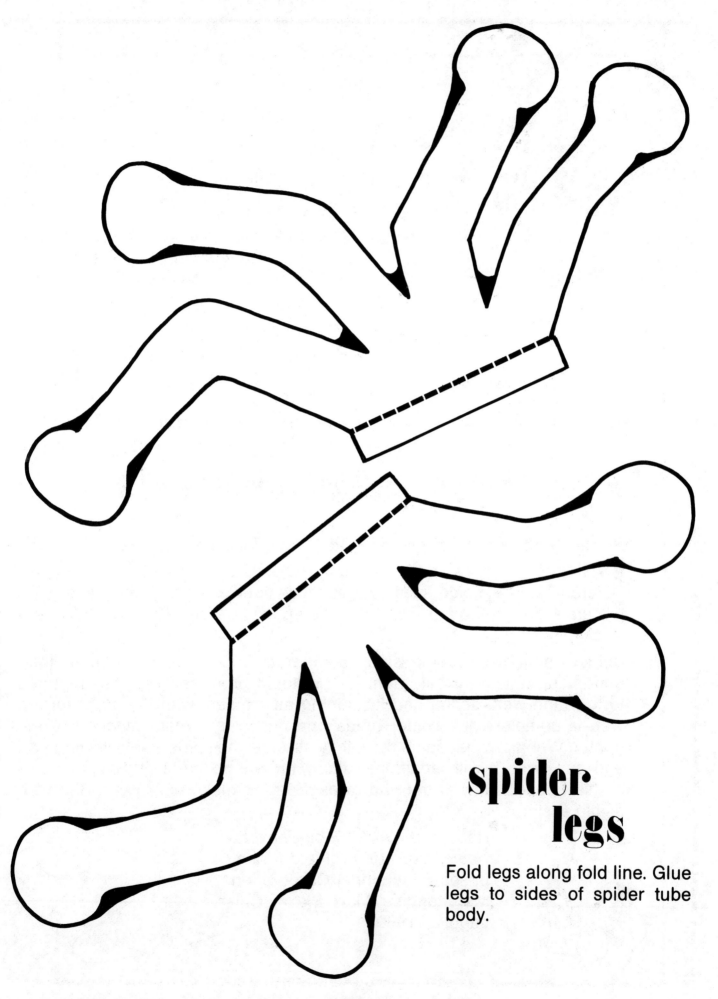

spider legs

Fold legs along fold line. Glue legs to sides of spider tube body.

GA1146

- Spiders are often confused with insects. Remember: Spiders have eight legs; insects have only six.
- Spiders do NOT have wings.
- Spiders have only two body parts: thorax (front part including the head and four pair of legs); abdomen (back section).
- Spiders are man's friend because they can kill harmful insects. Most spiders are nonpoisonous. Sometimes a spider will bite if it is in danger.

Amazing Arachnids

- Female spiders are usually given the credit for spinning webs. They also lay eggs.
- Different types of spiders spin various types of webs. They use these webs to catch food. Although the web may appear delicate, it is actually very strong.
- Spiders spin webs using small spinnerets located at the end of their abdomen, as well as silk glands. The liquid produced can be stretched to form the web, drying and hardening as it meets with the air. After the web is complete, the spider holds one end of a thread attached to the center. When prey lands on the sticky strands, the spider feels its vibration and can wrap it with additional sticky threads to catch it. Spiders have a little hooked claw at the end of each leg to make walking on the web a little easier.

Resource: *World Book Encyclopedia*, Vol. 16 S. Field Enterprises Educational Corporation. Merchandise Mart Plaza, Chicago, IL, 1960.

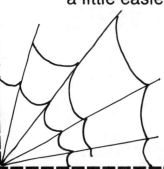

GA1146

1

Fill your classroom with a variety of materials about spiders: pictures, magazine articles, filmstrips, fiction and nonfiction books to use for reference. Read books to your class. Teach them songs about spiders.

2

Spin a story. Make a story web. First draw a large web on scrap paper. In the center of the web, print the word *spider*. In the other spaces, write down words related to a spider. Use the words to create a story.

Amazing Arachnid

3

Create a spider museum.
1. Have children catch a live spider.
2. Create a habitat to keep the spider alive.
3. Identify the spider.
4. Research and write a brief report.
5. Display the spider report in the museum.

4

Use the puppet you created to dramatize different situations in a spider's life. These might include spinning a web, spider catching prey, spider meeting spider, or spider hatching.

GA1146

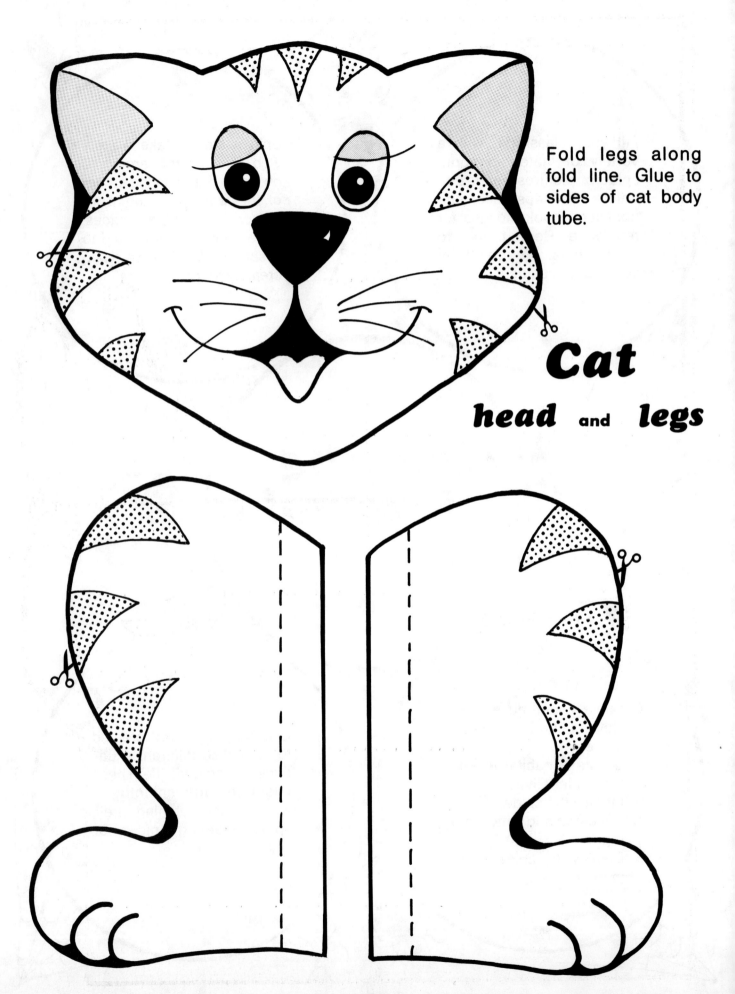

Fold legs along fold line. Glue to sides of cat body tube.

Cat

head and legs

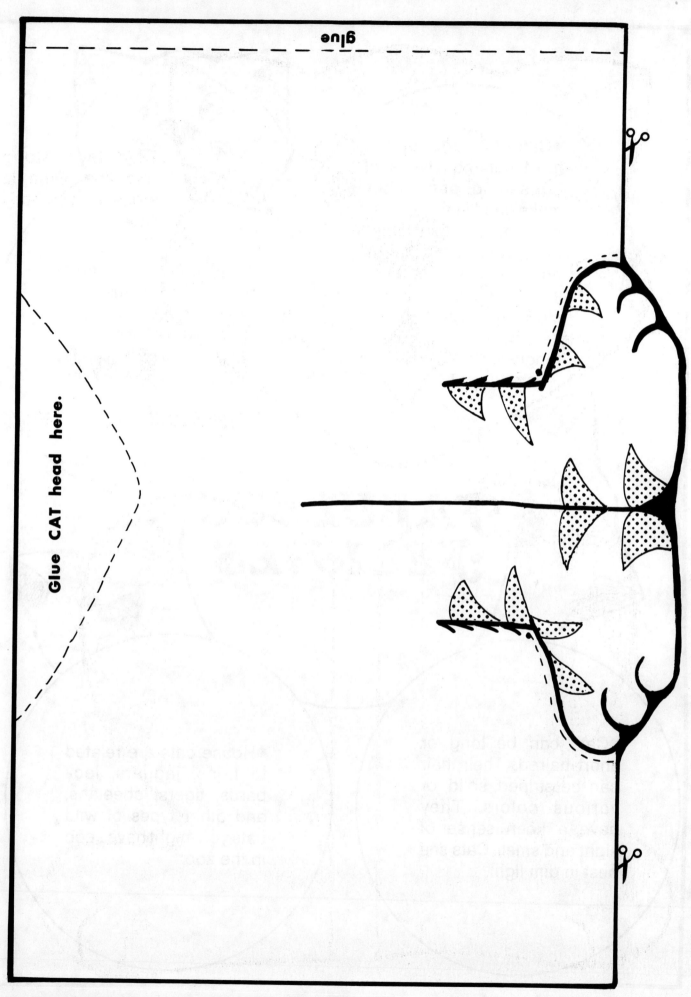

glue

Glue CAT head here.

129

● Cats are one of the most common types of household pets. They make good pets because they are intelligent mammals and learn to be quite independent. They also keep themselves clean by licking themselves with their tongues.

● Cats can be very helpful to man because they are clever hunters, using their sharp teeth and claws to kill harmful mice and other small rodents.

FABULOUS FELINES

● Cats can be long or short-haired. Their hair can be striped, solid, or various colors. They have a keen sense of sight and smell. Cats see best in dim light.

● House cats are related to lions, jaguars, leopards, tigers, cheetahs, and other types of wild cats you might have seen in the zoo.

GA1146

Fabulous Felines

1. 35
+ 17

2. 64
+ 29

3. 76
+ 34

4. 78
+ 56

5. 136
+ 254

6. 209
+ 835

7. 583
+ 708

8. 257
+ 462

9. 123
+ 295

10. 485
+ 155

11. 3524
+ 4068

12. 9572
+ 4583

13. 7609
+ 1357

14. 2054
+ 9683

15. 9876
+ 5609

GA1146

OWL

face

and

wings

Cut BEAK along
dotted lines
and fold outward.

Fold WINGS on dotted
lines. Glue to OWL body.

132

GA1146

OWL body

Glue OWL face here. Do NOT glue beak.

glue

GA1146

WHOO GIVES A HOOT ?

- The owl's appearance might account for the fact that it is often referred to as a wise animal. Its long eyelashes accentuate its large eyes, which are fixed in a forward position, as though it is concentrating on a task.

- To see behind them, owls can turn their entire heads around. Their stocky bodies are covered with dull feathers to disguise them. Sometimes the tufts of feathers on the top of their heads are mistaken for ears, which are small openings *under* the feathers.

- Owls eat mostly mammals, live prey whenever possible. Their sharp claws and pointed, hooked beaks make this job a little easier. Sometimes they catch prey in their mighty feet and carry it to a perch for feasting.

- Because owls are not skilled home builders, they often live in deserted structures or in hollow trees.

- Owls are referred to as nocturnal or night birds. That is the time they prefer to do their hunting and other such activities.

134

GA1146

WHOO HOOTS ?

1

Can you solve the riddle?
Read each question and circle the correct answers.

		YES	NO
1.	Owls hunt at night.	N	P
2.	Owls are birds.	O	X
3.	Owls build great nests.	R	C
4.	Owls are dull colored.	T	A
5.	Owls live in groups.	E	U
6.	Owls have fur.	S	R
7.	Owls never use their feet.	L	N
8.	Owls eat mammals.	A	Y
9.	Owls can turn their heads completely around.	L	K

Owls are _____ animals.

2

How many words can you make from *nocturnal*?

1. _____
2. _____
3. _____
4. _____
5. _____
6. _____
7. _____
8. _____
9. _____

3

```
S R E H T A E F
O A I Z L E X R V I
D J B E A K I W G J
U R E T N U H B S U
L T I K R N I W E S
L D S B U Q A O Y X
J L A H T L T S E N
E H W S C Z E V R L
A T O O H G F E
E T N O T G
```

4

Scrambled Words

1. TOHO _____
2. KAEB _____
3. LWSAC _____
4. UTRENH _____
5. TEAFSREH _____
6. LANRUTCON _____
7. LOW _____
8. BDRI _____
9. SEEY _____

Find the words above in the word hunt on the left. Circle them.

135

GA1146

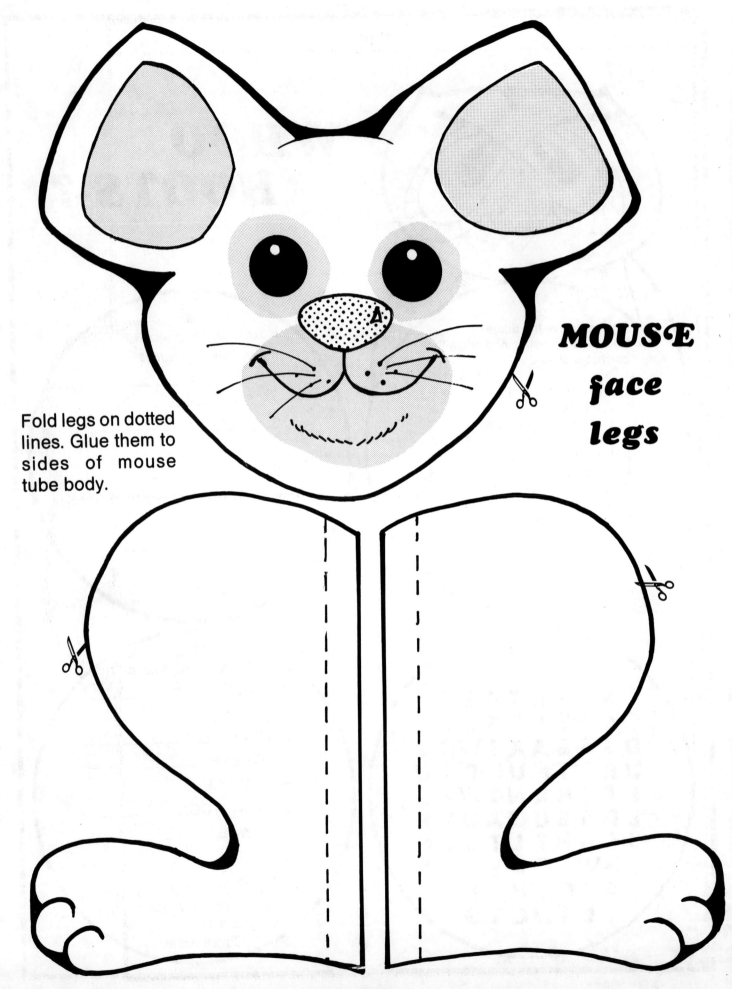

Fold legs on dotted lines. Glue them to sides of mouse tube body.

MOUSE
face
legs

A

136

GA1146

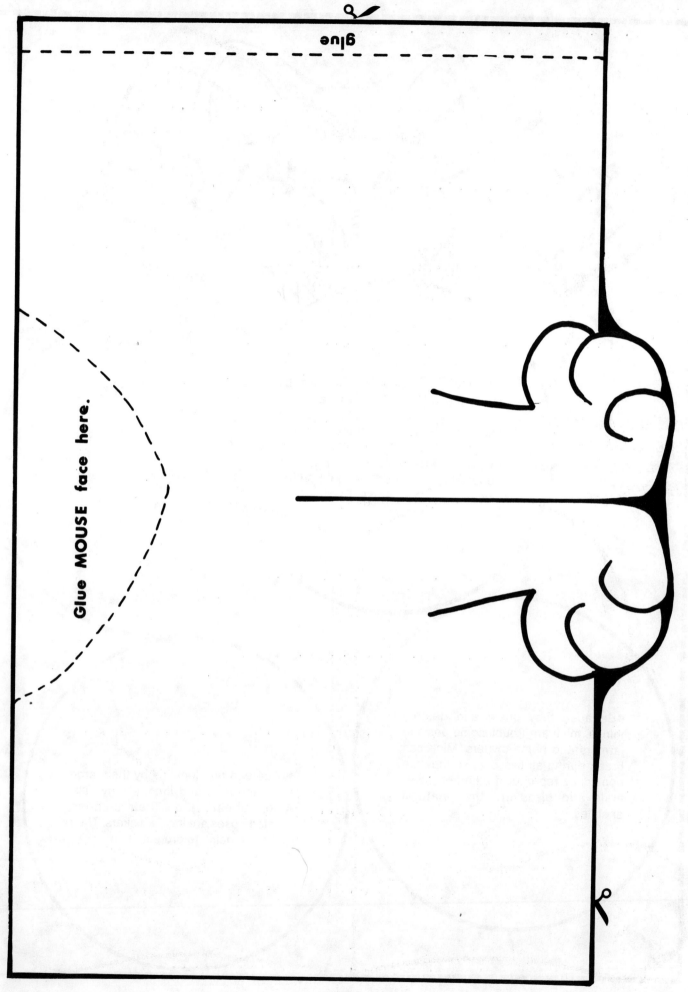

glue

Glue MOUSE face here.

137

GA1146

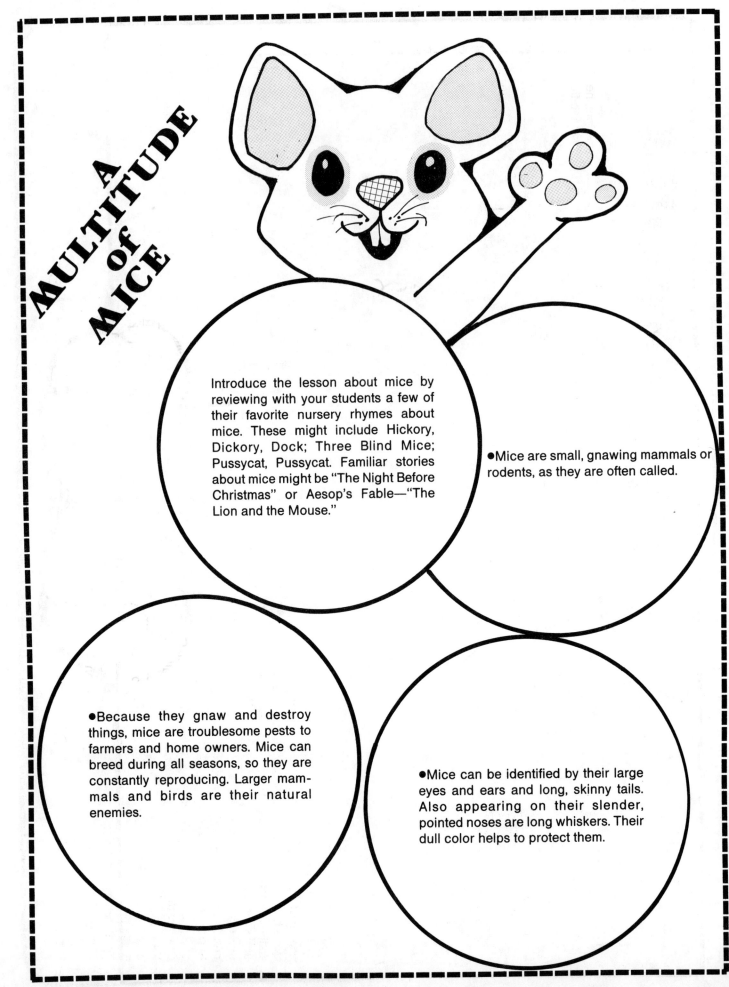

A MULTITUDE of MICE

Introduce the lesson about mice by reviewing with your students a few of their favorite nursery rhymes about mice. These might include Hickory, Dickory, Dock; Three Blind Mice; Pussycat, Pussycat. Familiar stories about mice might be "The Night Before Christmas" or Aesop's Fable—"The Lion and the Mouse."

● Mice are small, gnawing mammals or rodents, as they are often called.

● Because they gnaw and destroy things, mice are troublesome pests to farmers and home owners. Mice can breed during all seasons, so they are constantly reproducing. Larger mammals and birds are their natural enemies.

● Mice can be identified by their large eyes and ears and long, skinny tails. Also appearing on their slender, pointed noses are long whiskers. Their dull color helps to protect them.

138

GA1146

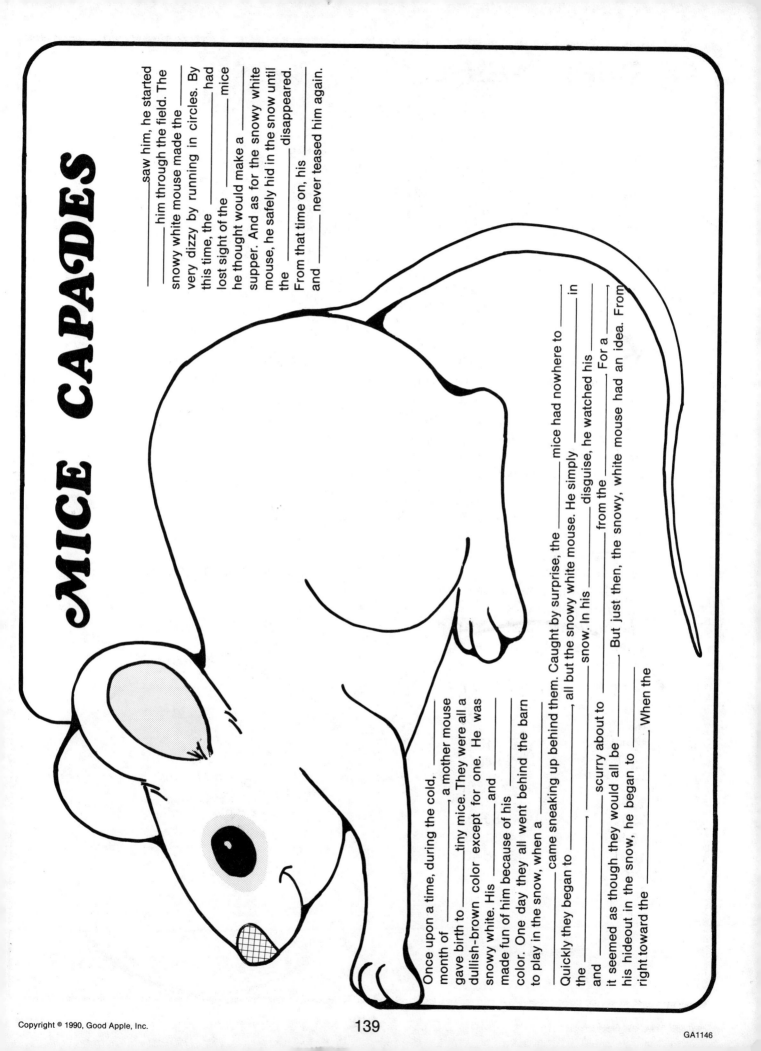

MICE CAPADES

_____ saw him, he started _____ him through the field. The snowy white mouse made the very dizzy by running in circles. By this time, the _____ had _____ lost sight of the _____ mice he thought would make a _____ supper. And as for the snowy white mouse, he safely hid in the snow until the _____ disappeared. From that time on, his _____ and _____ never teased him again.

Once upon a time, during the cold, _____ month of _____ a mother mouse gave birth to _____ tiny mice. They were all a dullish-brown color except for one. He was _____ and _____ snowy white. His _____ made fun of him because of his color. One day they all went behind the barn to play in the snow, when a _____ came sneaking up behind them. Caught by surprise, the _____ mice had nowhere to _____ in _____ all but the snowy white mouse. He simply _____ disguise, he watched his _____ snow. In his _____ from the _____ For a _____ scurry about to _____ But just then, the snowy, white mouse had an idea. From _____ it seemed as though they would all be _____ his hideout in the snow, he began to _____ When the _____ right toward the _____

GA1146

Answer Key

Page 45
1. turtle 2. 2 3. lamb 4. C2, D2 5. * 6.*
7. three baby chicks 8. * 9. B8 10. *
11. D3 12. E3 13. * 14. hen, baby chick
15. C6, D6, C5, D5, E5, C4, D4, E4

Page 49
1. Ham Burger 2. Ketchup, Lettuce, Mayonnaise, Cheese, Tomato, Seasoning, Onions, Pickles, Relish, Mustard 3. Sesame Seedlings Forest 4. Yellow 5. Sweet 6. Cheese 7. 200 8. 800 9. Cheddar to Longhorn 10. 900 11. Dill to Yellow 12. 800 13. Tomato and Relish 14. 900 15. Romaine to Whipped 16. Cheese 17. Colby and Whipped or Saucy and Romaine 18. 1000 19. Lettuce, Mayonnaise, Tomato 20. Relish

Page 95 (Accept any reasonable answer.)
1. To keep birds and other harmful pests away from crops
2. Wood, cloth, metal, plastic, rope
3. Answers will vary.
4. Insecticides, biological agents, chemicals, genetic breeding
5. Drawing
6. Drawing

Page 131
1. 52
2. 93
3. 110
4. 134
5. 390
6. 1044
7. 1291
8. 719
9. 418
10. 640
11. 7592
12. 14, 155
13. 8966
14. 11,737
15. 15,485

Page 135
1. hoot
2. beak
3. claws
4. hunter
5. feathers
6. nocturnal
7. owl
8. bird
9. eyes

How many words can you make from *nocturnal*? (Answers will vary.)

Can you solve the riddle?
1. N
2. O
3. C
4. T
5. U
6. R
7. N
8. A
9. L
Owls are *nocturnal* animals.

GA1146